Annie M. Lawrence

Light
From the Cross

Revised for today's readers
by
Diane Joy Truitt

Light From the Cross

Orginally published in the United States by D. Lothrop & Co., 1869, under the title of *Light From the Cross*.

Copyright © 2001
Diane Joy Truitt
All rights reserved
This edition has been edited for the modern reader, with much of the 1900th century spoken language translated for easier comprehension.

Allegheny Publications
ISBN 0-938037-02-1

Printed by
Allegheny Publications
2161 Woodsdale Road
Salem, OH 44460

Table of Contents

Chapter I	*Lucy Day and the New Scholar*	5
Chapter II	*Plans of Life*	11
Chapter III	*Mary Bradley's Sunday*	19
Chapter IV	*Beginning School Life*	26
Chapter V	*Breaking of the Day*	32
Chapter VI	*A Christian Home*	41
Chapter VII	*Joy in Labor for Others*	51
Chapter VIII	*Temptation and Triumph*	58
Chapter IX	*A Merry Christmas*	72
Chapter X	*Forgiveness and It's Fruits*	82

Chapter XI
Shadows and Sunshine   *97*

Chapter XII
Toiling for the Brave   *117*

Chapter XIII
Reaping the Harvest   *129*

Chapter XIV
Conclusion   *150*

Light From the Cross

Chapter I
Lucy Day and the New Scholar

It was four o'clock in Lucy Day's schoolroom. Dinner-baskets and books, with their respective owners, were rapidly disappearing, till at last the oft-repeated words, "Good-by, teacher," were all said, and the happy voices of the little flock died away in the distance, and Lucy was left alone. That the day had been one of unusual weariness was plainly shown in the pale cheeks and heavy eyes of the young teacher. It was one of those days that fall to the lot of every instructor, when many trifling annoyances so multiplied themselves as to render what were usually pleasant duties weary tasks.

"Please, lady, the minister sent you this," aroused her from the day-dream into which she had fallen, and with a start of surprise, she quickly turned to view the intruder. A child of perhaps ten years, though the weary look on her young face added still other years to her appearance, was thin and pale, ragged, and not particularly clean. There was a strange yearning look in the eyes that looked into her own so earnestly. After taking the letter, which the child held toward her, she pleasantly said "Thank you, my dear." The kind words won a faint smile to the sad mouth of her little visitor and thus Lucy silently proceeded to read through the contents of the letter while the child sat down near, her gaze riveted on the face of the lady. The letter ran thus:

My Dear Young Lady,

    Your scholars say that you are the best teacher in the wide world, and are never tired of telling of your kindness to them. Acting on this constantly repeated information, I take the liberty to introduce the bearer of this as a claimant on your sympathy. I should have seen you personally, but am obliged to leave home today, for an absence of a month or more. This little girl, Mary Bradley, will tell you her story, if you desire to hear it; and some ladies in the neighborhood are fitting her with decent clothing so that she can attend Sabbath and day schools. It is best you should understand her case if she is to attend your school, and I would advise you to question her at the earliest opportunity. God bless you in your duties, and make them a labor of love for Him.

Yours in Christ,
Pastor Adams

    Silently as she had read, so silently did Lucy return the note to its envelope, then she held out her hand to the child, who came timidly forward and stood by her side.

    "And so your name is Mary," she said pleasantly, hardly knowing how to commence the conversation, or ask for the story that the little girl was evidently waiting to impart.

    "Yes'm, Mary Bradley, and I'm going to come to school here, so the minister said."

    "You like Pastor Adams, the minister?" Lucy questioned.

    A quick flush crimsoned Mary's face as she answered, "Like him! He's the best friend I ever had in the world, and he said," and the girl's look grew wonderfully pleading in its earnestness, "he said he thought you would be my friend, too, and I shall be so glad, for I hadn't got many."

    "I hope I shall be your friend, my poor child," Lucy answered, "but won't you tell me where you live, and if you have any parents?"

    The faint smile that had played fitfully over the sad, young face faded

Lucy Day and the New Scholar

away, and a look almost of shame cast its shadow thereon.

"He said I must tell you my story, but I do hate to, though I'm not to blame. He said nobody that was as good as they say you are, lady, would say I was one bit to blame. But I don't love to tell anything about it."

"If it grieves you so, we will wait till some other time," said Lucy kindly, "sometime when you and I have got better acquainted."

"No. I was to tell you tonight," she said firmly, "unless I shall make you tired," saying as an afterthought that perhaps she was intruding. The native delicacy showing itself in look and tone won still more of Lucy's attention and sympathy, and she gave the assurance that she was by no means tired.

"Will you take hold of my hand while I'm talking?" was the next question. "I washed my hands clean so as not to soil the letter, and somehow I feel as if I could talk better."

So the little brown hand nestled in that of her newly found friend, and the story was told, a story that filled the listener's heart with sincere pity.

Her father, years before, had killed her mother in a drunken quarrel, and had been sentenced to serve a term of years in prison from where he had but just been released. Having taken his child from the alms-house where her life had been spent since her mother's death and his imprisonment they had come to Martinsville where Lucy was teaching. There he found an empty house, or rather a crude cabin, on the outskirts of the village, and had obtained permission to occupy it as long as he could find means to pay the small rent demanded.

Little Mary had, most of the time, been kindly treated at the alms-house. The change from the well-cooked and abundant, even if coarse meals, to the still coarser and badly prepared food of which she was now obliged to partake, would have been a trial had no other cause for grief existed. Yet she had other trials, harder still.

Naturally irritable, Stephen Bradley's prison life, with all its shame and disgrace, and the still more shameful and ever-present recollection that the one who best love, he might almost have said, the only one who ever really loved him, had met her death at his hand. The thought of all this, with no hope of earthly or heavenly joy, had rendered him morose and sullen beyond description. Rejecting society, only so far as he was obliged to accept it in his daily work, he had likewise tried to seclude his child from all companionship with those around. Only after the most persistent and judicious efforts, had the minister of Martinsville, Pastor Adams, obtained his permission to have the child attend the village school, and also the Sabbath school connected with his church.

Only glimpses and outlines of this came to Lucy Day's knowledge from little Mary's faltering told story, but enough was comprehended to enlist the lady's sympathy towards the worse than orphan child.

"And when are you to commence coming to school?" she inquired as she bade Mary goodnight.

"Next Monday, Pastor Adams said," and with almost a joyful look, the girl added, "I'm going Church and to Sunday school too, like other folks."

"Poor child!" thought Lucy, "what are my trials to hers, and yet I complain."

While walking home, through her mind, like a flash, shone the truth that one of God's ways to comfort us in grief is by sending other sorrowful ones to us for sympathy and cheer. The longer she thought the more earnestly did she desire to aid in brightening the life of this sad little one.

Lucy paused for a moment to chat with Widow Brewer, who, seated in her armchair under a rustic porch, was enjoying the close of the day. The subject of her thoughts continued from Mrs. Brewer's remarks, commenced by the question,

"Was that Stephen Bradley's little girl with you just now?"

"Yes, can you tell me anything about her, or her father?" queried Lucy.

"Poor child! Poor little forsaken lamb!" went on the old lady, "she hasn't the bright, rosy look that her mother had, when she was at her age. Mary Lisle was a pretty girl, merry, loving and willful and an only child. She was praised and indulged in every whim and wish, till they came nigh spoiling her. She ruled the household just after her own notions, and some of them were pretty whimsical ones, I assure you."

Lucy Day and the New Scholar

Lucy settled herself composedly on the doorstep, for, in her walks past Mrs. Brewer's cottage, she had learned the old lady's style of conversation, and loved dearly to listen to her stories of days gone by. Which had ever this peculiar charm—everything pleasant seemed to grow constantly more beautiful in the light of her loving memory, while all things disagreeable shrank almost to nothingness and left no bitterness behind. So the sweet old voice kept on the thread of the story:

"When she grew older, Mary Lisle had plenty of admirers, some of them the likeliest young men in the township, but her heart seemed fixed on Stephen Bradley, and have him she would, in spite of parents and all her friends said against him. He was a good fellow to work, but he would have his sprees. Once Mary's father brought him home from another town, too drunk to know what he was about. But he was so penitent and made such fair promises that Mary forgave him, and at last they were married, and lived in that white cottage next to Dr. Osborne's. For six months he did nicely, and everybody thought he had really reformed, and would make a good citizen, now, as they said, 'he had sowed all his wild oats.'

"Mary was the picture of happiness, and used often to rally her friends on her wisdom in marrying to please herself. I had a daughter about her age, and she and Mary were always great friends. One night Ellen, that was my girl's name, went over to see Mary, and when she came home, which she did pretty soon, I saw as plain as day that something was the matter. And there was, sure enough. Stephen had been to a great gathering, and had come home the worse for liquor. He was not cross, but dreadfully silly and Ellen said she could not stay and see Mary's shame and grief at his appearance. After that time he seemed to go down hill fast, and nothing Mary could say made any difference. He had said, months before, that he didn't want any help to keep him from evil habits that he could take care of himself. It has always seemed to me that God left him to his own weakness that he might learn the need of divine aid to guide and uphold.

"However it was, he went from bad to worse. Before Mary had been married two years, and when her baby was a few months old, he came home one day with one of his drinking companions, and getting angry over their cards and glasses, they were soon in a terrible fight. Mary darted forward to plead with her husband, when he raised a heavy chair to strike his companion, and turning in a rage to her on account of her meddling, she received the full force of the blow and fell dead at his feet. Both men were sobered right away, and they say that neither of them had touched a drop of liquor since. I didn't believe Stephen would live his sentence out. He was so crushed by grief and remorse, but he did, and what seems strange, has come right back here to live. He doesn't look much as he used to, and acts, as Squire Atherton said the other day, as though peace and hope had died out of his heart and life. Somehow I think he is trusting in his own strength yet, and never thinks of God's pity and help."

"I pity that poor little girl," said Lucy, softly.

"Aye, so do I, poor lamb!" Replied Mrs. Brewer. "And I pity Stephen, too, and I can't help having faith to believe that the time will come when he will find peace in forgiveness through Christ. Perhaps that child will be the means, in God's hands, of accomplishing good, by winning him to seek salvation. There have been too many prayers offered for him, to have him live all his life away from the true light."

Golden sunbeams crept in through the wreaths of honeysuckle shading the porch, for a last smile, brightening the placid face of the dear old lady, as Lucy looked up with low-spoken words,

"I wish I had your faith to believe our prayers will surely be answered. I try so hard always to do right, and fail so often. I pray for blessings, and they don't come, sometimes I'm almost tempted to give it all up. Why, all this trying to be good and do good, I don't seem to progress at all, sometimes I feel as though I'm growing worse instead of better."

Lucy spoke earnestly, and her eyes glistened with tears. Mrs. Brewer's next question came almost comfortless to her tried spirit,

"My dear girl, are you trusting in Christ's mercy, or your own good works?" for she knew then how weak the anchor of her spirit's hope was.

Chapter II
Plans of Life

ll that evening, and the next day, Lucy Day's thoughts had two new subjects for consideration, the little stranger, and good Mrs. Brewer's parting question.

The oldest daughter of a large family, who had never known the real want of a needed comfort, till sudden misfortune stripped them of their wealth. The disaster left Lucy to help herself by the labor of her own hands, this school at Martinsville was her first attempt at teaching, and she was succeeding even better than she had hoped.

Her parents were worldly people, who, if they went to church once on Sunday, and opened and read from the Bible weekly, considered their religious duties adequately performed. Accustomed from her childhood to listen, at church and Sabbath school, to the doctrine that Christ's mission was simply that of a teacher and guide, she had been thrown, since her sojourn in Martinsville, under the influence of far different teachings. She had felt keenly her father's loss of property, but had tried to school herself to a philosophic if not patient endurance of her trials.

"How can you be so calm, and even cheerful, Lucy?" asked Laura Howard, her most intimate friend, when the first shock of disaster had passed away from the Day family, and they were beginning to lay plans for the future. "I should give right up, I know, and drift down with the current. 'Tis too bad that this has happened; for, however dearly we who know you best will always love you, there will be those who will look down upon you if you work for your own living."

"What would you have me do, Laura? Sit down idly and starve?" Lucy tried to laugh, but her heart was heavy, and she added, half as though talking to herself, "All I hope for just now is, that I shall have strength to keep up, and show myself undaunted by misfortune. I don't mean people shall know if I do feel badly. If sorrow is a good discipline for maturing and beautifying the character, perhaps it's sent to me for a wise purpose. I know I can accomplish something in the world, and I mean to, if I live."

"That's it, Lu," called out a hearty voice near them, for the two girls had overlooked the possibility of listeners, and were talking in earnest tones. "You're a trump, keep up a stiff upper lip, and you'll come out all right," and the speaker, Laura's danger-daring, fun-loving brother, pushed aside the green canopy that shaded them, and threw himself on the grass beside the girls. "Only I beg of you," he went on, " not to get into the notion of drawing down your face, and, as old Miss Peters says, 'nursing' your trials, because you imagine you've done some terrible thing, and that all this is sent to you as a punishment, that's all fudge.

"I don't know, perhaps I need punishing," Lucy said, a good deal amused at Harry Howard's dictatorial manner.

"Well, so we all do, but we don't all have trouble, at least Laura and I don't, we are just as merry as bob-o-links in a clover-field, and we certainly deserve punishing as much as you do, if not more. I believe in folks being spunky, and keeping a stiff upper lip, but this everlastingly droning about trials being a just retribution, and our having such weak, erring natures, and needing sorrow to keep us straight, and all that, it's miserable nonsense. At least that's my opinion, and you may have it for what it's worth."

"Quite a sermon," laughed Laura. "But I would like to have you go on a little farther, and tell us what troubles are sent for?"

"Sent? Just because they happen to come, I suppose just so much evil is mixed up with the good, and in distributing both, some people get all, and they may be fitly termed lucky, some get a mixture, and get along very well. While others get evil, pure, unadulterated evil, and they must grin and bear it, as best they can, and wait for the next turn of the wheel of fortune to bring a better state of things. That's Howard philosophy, young ladies."

"I can't say that I just agree with you," Lucy replied. "I think we can all do a great deal towards making our own happiness or misery, and I am more than half a convert to the theory that all evil brings its own punishment, and that all sorrow comes as a just reward for wrongs committed. I hope I shall receive meekly whatever comes, and have strength to do my duty, and live a life of carefulness in all that is right."

Poor girl! She little knew that her assumption of meekness was but a thin veil, failing to cover the great pride and boastful self-reliance of her heart.

"Well, well, have it as you please," yawned Harry lazily, "but allow me to give you a text on which to found the sermon of your future career, to wit, these lines:

> 'Oh, faint not in a world like this,
> And thou shalt know ere long,
> Know how sublime a thing it is
> To suffer and be strong.'"

"I hope I shall," answered Lucy, "at any rate, as I said before, I mean to be strong. I *can* be patient, and I *will* be, I *can* be of some use in the world, and I *will* be. If I can't be happy, at least people shall think I am, and Martinsville shall have a faithful teacher, on that I am fully determined."

"Hold the reins tight, little woman," Harry threw back the words laughingly, and went his way, and the two girls were left alone. Neither seemed in the mood for having the long talk, which they had planned to enjoy this last afternoon, that they were to spend together.

The soft, hazy September atmosphere lay over the landscape, here and there a solitary tree burned with crimson or gleamed out in golden richness, but most of the forests yet wore the livery of summer. The numberless musical sounds of insect life filled the air with slumberous harmony, and the glitter and purl of the meadow-stream that showed itself like a silver ribbon edged with green added a great deal to the charm of the scenery lying bright before them.

Laura was thinking how beautifully Picnic Grove looked on the hillside, over beyond the brook, and how fair the prospect was for a happy time there the coming week, wishing Lucy could be there to enjoy the pleasure with her. Meanwhile Lucy was wishing she could know just how she should succeed in her new duties as teacher, and wondering, too, when she should again see the dear old familiar scenes that were spread out before her.

Harry's words, in their cheery, bantering tones, had roused a new train of thought, and she wondered if, after all, things didn't sometimes just happen, instead of being really the working of an all-wise, far-seeing Providence.

"A penny for your thoughts, Lucy," Laura roused her.

"I hardly think they are worth even that much," she answered. "I was only trying to solve that great problem, the whys and wherefores of life, and as usual met with a puzzle. I have heard it said that we can make our lives just what we please. Last night I was reading a story, and I came across this quotation from Feuerbach, 'Every being is sufficient to itself, that is, every being is, in and by itself, infinite.' I wonder if it is so."

"I don't pretend to understand such matters," returned her friend, "I should think, however, such an assertion would have to be taken in a restricted sense. Exceptions to the rule there must be, for I'm certain I never should imagine myself possessing infinite strength. I make no pretensions."

"And then, besides," Lucy added, seemingly unconscious of Laura's words, "I got a volume of Emerson's Essays from the Library the other day. I heard the doctor and Mr. Gardner talking about the book, and I wanted to see it. I find it full of such ideas as this: 'If we take the good we find, asking no questions, we shall have heaping measures. Everything good is on the highway.' And again, 'Our life seems not present, so much as prospective, not for the affairs on which it is wasted, but as a hint of this vast-flowing vigor. Most of life seems to be mere advertisement of faculty.' Now if this be so, I mean to improve upon it, and make my life something more than an advertisement, and come what will, be strong in and of myself."

"I hope you'll do all, and more than you have planned, and I've faith to believe that you will, you know 'tis said, 'God helps those who help themselves.' It was a truth that, lightly spoken as it was, rested itself theoretically on a surer foundation than Lucy's pride-nurtured resolves. The conversation drifted into other channels.

This was almost a year previous to the date of our last chapter. Her resolves for a self-sustained and never-to-be-daunted perseverance had oftentimes proved hindrances instead of helps, and galling chains instead of a supporting staff. She was fast learning her own weakness, but drifting with the current of her chosen ideas, she saw not the kind hand reaching from the shore to give her the aid she needed.

Mrs. Brewer had taken an interest in her, from the time of her first coming to Martinsville, partly because of Lucy's many little attentions constantly shown the aged lady. Indeed they were towards all with whom the young girl came in contact, and in part because she guessed the unreliable source of Lucy's strength. More than once she had been on the point of coming directly to the subject, and making an effort to win her confidence on the great matter of her soul's inner life. Except something, she never could tell exactly what, had seemed to compel her silence. Of late she had more than half begun to realize that Lucy possessed a certain craftiness in changing the theme of conversation whenever it approached disputed points in religion or tended to induce any close examination of the hidden springs of life. The good lady offered many prayers for her young friend and watched for opportunities to speak the right word in the right place. Such an opportunity offered itself, when she probed Lucy's motives by the question, "Are you trusting in Christ's mercy, or in your own good works?"

The question repeated itself to Lucy one night when she sat through the long hours by the side of one of her pupils who was seriously ill. It had been her settled purpose, when she left home, to seek for openings for doing others a kindness, to win all around to love her, to mold her life into a perfect round of goodness and beauty. Sadly she tried without that right spring of action, the glory of God, and she found oftentimes weariness instead of comforting rest in her efforts and their results. That night, in her inner self, she was ready to exclaim, as has more than one tried spirit, "Oh, for a rest in the grave! For life is but an empty show." She was universally beloved, and as home reports told of health, prosperity and happiness, her griefs and discomforts arose alone from her own spirit.

The weak voice of the little sufferer aroused her from her thoughts. Unwittingly the child's question fitted itself into her train of thought:

"Miss Day, what does this mean? I learned a verse to say at church last Sunday, but I was too sick to go, so I didn't say it. I don't quite know what it means."

"What is the verse, dear?" asked Lucy, not at all sure of the propriety of permitting the child to talk, and yet glad of something that broke the tiresome silence of thought.

"'Tis this: 'By grace are ye saved, through faith, and that not of yourselves, it is the gift of God.'"

"And what troubles you in this verse, Bessie?" Lucy was herself puzzled how to make plain to the child what she did not understand.

"Why, I learned a few weeks ago, that we must 'work out our own salvation with fear and trembling.' This says the same as to tell us it is nothing of ourselves, but the gift of God. Mother brought in Grandpa's commentary today to read it all out to me, but the baby cried so she had to go out of the room. I thought perhaps that you would tell me. I can't get to sleep, and 'twill make me feel better if you talk to me, teacher."

"Is the commentary here now?" Lucy saw a gleam of light before her, and gladly hailed it.

"I believe Mother put it on the table over there, and I shall love to hear you read. Uncle George says, just what I think, too, that your reading is sweeter music than some people's singing."

Lucy kissed the little flushed face and went for the commentary, and having found the verse, she asked, "Do you know, Bessie, what faith means?"

"Mother says," answered the child, "that 'tis believing is not being afraid, and feeling as sure that things will happen, just as God has told us in the Bible, as though we saw them happening before us."

"Yes, Bessie, and it says here that 'our faith, or conversion, and our eternal salvation, are not from any natural powers of our own, or any merit of our own, but all and everything comes from God, from His free goodness, and merciful favor. But faith and the fruits of faith are His gift. We are unable to help ourselves, but all this wonderful change that makes us Christians, comes to us through the riches of His grace.'"

Bessie listened attentively, a quiet look creeping over her face, and as Lucy paused, she asked, "And what does 'work out your own salvation' mean?"

Lucy turned over the pages till she found the place, and then, half reading, half explaining, to make it clearer to her young hearer, she went on, "'To work out our own salvation means, working thoroughly, and taking great pains. Salvation is the greatest of all things, and we can not attain it without the utmost care and diligence.' Then, Bessie, you know it adds, 'with fear and trembling.' Fear is a great guard to preserve us from evil, for, you know, if we are afraid of anything, we are very careful to keep away from it, and it may mean also, not only lowliness of mind, but diligence and caution, and fear of displeasing."

"Please read on, dear teacher," pleaded Bessie, as Lucy paused, "it rests me ever so much."

"I am afraid you will be worse if you don't try to sleep," said Lucy, as she prepared the child's medicine and bathed her face and hands.

"Oh, no, Mother said if you was willing, I might ask you to read, it makes me feel ever so much better, the reading and everything you do."

So the book was again taken up, and the reading resumed, "'By the Holy Spirit, the mind is prepared and the heart redeemed to discern truth, and love holiness, and where we once chose evil, we now choose good, without the slightest infringement of our liberty. God has made over our desires, and from doing wrong we want to do right. This leads us to good works, or an employment of our powers for God's service, without weariness or fear, only a holy, child-like fear, that is only afraid of doing anything to displease so gracious and loving a Father. Good works come from love, not for love, from grace, not for grace.'"

"Yes," interrupted Bessie, "Mother told me about that. She said God gave us so freely the forgiveness of our sins, it was as if He made us over new creatures. Some people believe if we try to do everything just right that will save us, but He having done so much for us, we shall want to please Him. Grandpa heard her, and he said, 'Yes, good works follow salvation, not salvation the good works, they are only the pleasant plants that grow up around the fountain where our sins are washed away.' I thought that was beautiful, and so I remembered it. Will you sing, 'There is a fountain filled with blood?'" and while she sang, the child fell asleep, and Lucy was left again to the companionship of her own thoughts.

Little Bessie had been carefully taught, and was unusually thoughtful, and Lucy had more than once noticed in school the rapt attention, which she gave to the morning scriptural lesson, and to the repetition of the Lord's Prayer. Unwittingly, in explaining to the child, she had proved to her own mind how weak was the foundation on which she was building her own hopes. Lucy felt, as she walked home in the gray morning, as though, one by one, her hopes were fading, and the good and loving deeds that were to her stepping stones toward heaven, looked like a vain endeavor to cover the dangerous quagmire of sin, over which she seemed wandering.

"And yet," she said to herself, "I took Christ for my pattern, and have tried to follow Him, where could I look for a better guide?"

Poor girl! Her eyes were yet blinded, she wanted to follow Jesus, but in her own way, not His. She was still leaning on her own strength, not reaching up to the cross for support. She had yet to learn how sweet it is to feel that eternal salvation is sure only because Christ Jesus died; that in and through His death sinners might be pardoned.

Chapter III
Mary Bradley's Sunday

broad band of golden light lay far down in the east, when Mary Bradley opened her eyes that Sabbath morning which was to witness her introduction to the Sabbath school and the house of God. Few, and with long intervals between, had been the times when she had been allowed to attend church, there were so many older inmates of the alms-house who were anxious to go, it was seldom that there was an opportunity for her.

But today she was to be so happy, so she got up softly and lighted a fire in the old stove, shutting the door carefully, so as not to disturb her father, while she made the kitchen look as clean as she could, before she got breakfast. It seemed to her that she never saw anything half so beautiful as this morning.

"'Daylight cracking in the east,' Granny Ames used to say," she said to herself, every now and then running to the door to see how far and bright the golden glow deepened, "but this is more than a crack, it's the whole of the glory shining out at once. I wish Father would wake up and see it; too, I guess the birds like it, for they sing as if they would split their throats open. And the flowers are so sweet, I mean to go out and pick some, and have them on the table."

Mary had got into a habit of talking to herself, and a right sociable time she had, often whiling away many hours in this way, that would otherwise have been very lonely.

"Now that's pretty nosegay, I'm sure. My mug is just the thing to put it in. 'Twas real good of father to get it for me, and how glad I am we've got so nice a breakfast. It does seem as if everything was prettier and better this morning than ever before. Only I do wish," and she glanced at the rough table from which they were accustomed to eat, "I do wish I had a tablecloth, that table looks so bad. I don't know as father would like it, but there's that box of things he told me about the other day, when he felt good natured, that he said belonged to mother once, and that I am to have when I get bigger. I mean to see if I can't find a tablecloth in that, if it is unfastened. Luckily for the child, Mr. Bradley had opened the box the evening before, an unusual fit of tenderness prompting him to search for her mother's Bible that she might have it to carry to Sabbath school.

Several nice table-coverings rewarded her search, and taking one, which though a little yellow, looked as Mary expressed, "as good as other folk's." She proceeded to lay the table to the best of her ability, then she went and sat down in the doorway and waited for her father to rise. By and by she was thinking so attentively, wondering how it was that little "Red-hood," the woodpecker, could run on the underside of the limb and not tumble off, that she did not hear the bed-room door open and her father come out. His look of pleased surprise was followed by one of such remorseful sorrow, as would have grieved little Mary to see, but he turned before she looked up. When she saw him he looked as usual, only so pale that she thought he must be ill.

"Are you sick, father?" she questioned, earnestly, going towards him.

"No, no, child," he answered, "I feel well enough. What made you think I was sick? It isn't late, is it?"

"No, 'tis early, but you looked so white, you scared me. Don't things look nice? And father, I was thinking just now that I will try every day to make the house look real clean, and keep learning how to do and make things, and by and by I shall know enough to take care of the rooms as well anybody.

Little Mary was wholly in earnest. The sudden glow of excitement so transformed the pale young face, that she looked the image of her mother. When she went close beside her father, and throwing her arms around his

Mary Bradley's Sunday 21

neck, laid her soft cheek against his haggard one, the heart-softened man could only clasp her convulsively to his breast, while he shed such tears as only agony like his can wring out. Mary was frightened, she had never seen her father in such a mood before. But she felt certain he was not displeased with her, so she only nestled in her unusual resting-place, and kept her small hand smoothing away the hair from his forehead, till the man's passion of grief subsided, and he was calm enough to speak.

"My child, my poor, innocent child," he half whispered convulsively, "I have blasted your young life, and yet you love me."

"O, father, if you'll only let me!" said Mary, the flood-tide of affection surging over the wall of harshness and past neglect that had rendered the few months she had lived with her father the most miserable she had ever known. "I've been so hungry for love, and I thought you didn't care anything about me."

"I've been afraid to show that I loved you, my child. I thought you, like everybody else, despised me, but I won't neglect you any more, darling, and if I can't be happy, I will try to make you so."

Just then Mary remembered that time was flying. Breakfast wasn't eaten yet and she was to go over to Mrs. Lane's, and be dressed in her new garments for church.

"How I wish you was going, too father!" she said as she was starting, after what she declared had been the happiest breakfast she ever remembered.

"There's no room for me," the man answered, with something of his old gruffness. "I've no notion of going where I shall be scorned, unless I'm obliged to go. I don't think any one will be otherwise than kind to you, but there's many a one would forget they had met to worship God, if I should go among them. They despise me so. And who blames them?" he added, in sorrowful, but still bitter tones. "I deserve all, and more, too."

"Pastor Adams says, father," said Mary, her loving pity moving her to say something comforting, if possible, " if people are sorry for their sins, and ask God to forgive them, and they feel in their hearts that he has, and then they try with God's help to do what will please him, that he will make them happy. He said his love is better than that of any earthly friend."

Mr. Bradley did not reply, only to say "Good-bye." Mary was ready to go, then the child hastened over the fields to the nearest neighbor's. Two hours later, comfortably and neatly clothed, she followed Mrs. Lane up the aisle, and with beating heart took her seat.

Lucy Day saw Mary's newfound joy sending a flush to her cheeks and a light to her eyes that almost transformed her face. "What an interesting looking child!" thought Lucy. Old Mrs. Brewer and others who had known her mother said, "That is what Mary Lisle looked like!" At another time Mary Bradley might have been frightened, but just then, thought was so busy that she was unconscious of the many glances bestowed upon her.

A prayer was offered, a hymn sung, a portion of Scripture read, then another prayer winged its way to Heaven, and then followed the sweet and precious old hymn, "Rock of Ages."

A stranger occupied the desk, a quiet, scholarly looking man, who announced as his morning theme, "Salvation through Christ," founded on the text, "The blood of Jesus Christ, his Son cleanseth us from all sin."

"Far away in the East," he commenced, "many years ago, in the eastern part of the city of Jerusalem, in all its glory and splendor, rose the walls and pinnacles of that great temple. It was the time for the morning sacrifice and in great throngs came the people up through the beautiful and massive gates, into the great court, beyond which none but Jews might go. In cloudy fragrance rose, wave above wave, the smoke from the golden altar of incense.

"Beyond the court of Israel, nearest the sanctuary, within the court of the priests, stood the great altar of burnt-offering, where God commanded, were laid the sacrifices, prompted by a desire to avert the consequences of the guilt of sin. The priest would lay the sacrifice on the altar, making atonement for the person offering the sacrifice, whose meaning could be naught less than that of an atoning sacrifice for his sin. It was expiation for the soul, solemnly ordained and consecrated by the Lord, with the design of calling to remembrance the existence of sin. Blood flowing around the altar was symbolic in how guilt was washed away.

"Thus had God appointed, and so, day by day, the offerings were made, and in the blood of lambs and of bullocks the priest made the sacrifice of atonement for the sins of the people.

"But by and by came a time when a richer offering was needed, and was freely made. In the fullness of God's own time the sacrifice was laid upon the altar, and thenceforward, through all time, the great brazen altar needed no new gift. Christ dying on the cross thus had done away with the continual sacrifice of animals. Seconds after his death at Calvary, the sacred temple veil which separates the holy of holies, God's dwelling place, was rent from top to bottom. Thus letting worshipers know they can now come to God without the aid of a priest or the slaying of sacrifices. On the altar of divine justice, the Lamb of God had wrought out a full and everlasting expiation, for all who seek forgiveness and eternal salvation through him. His blood had flowed, and as the blood of the sacrifices flowing around the altar set forth the washing away of the guilt of sin, so the shedding of Christ's blood takes from the penitent soul the filthiness of transgression. His blood washes away our sins and according to scripture he remembers them no more.

"To the sin-stained and guilt-burdened soul redemption can come in no other way. There is no remission of sins without redemption, and we are held captive as by sin, whose chains bind us as prisoners. Thus held captive, there comes no release save by remission, this redemption through His blood. And this great, this priceless benefit comes freely to us, dearly bought and amply paid for, by our precious Redeemer, the Lord Jesus Christ. And yet it is only according to the riches of God's grace. God might have executed the full severity of the law on the transgressor, and it was grace, rich grace alone, that could think of providing such a surety as His own Son, such a glorious and pure substitute for fallen humanity. OH, the height and the depth and the unbounded breadth of the love and mercy, that could plan so rich and full a pardon, and lay up such an inheritance of blessedness through Him, the blessed One, who died and rose again! 'Tis wonderful, and yet so simple, 'tis a mystery, yet it shines forth the Word of truth and the Gospel of salvation, the glad tiding that shall be to all nations, and peoples, and tongues, the promise and the earnest of the joys laid up for them. And it all comes through Christ and His cross; there is no other name whereby we may be saved.

"Many and various have been the schemes that man in his ignorant pride has formed to win a place among the saints, and gain an inheritance with the heirs of heaven, but they are all useless, there is no climbing up by any other way. Christ only is the door, and no man cometh unto the Father save by Him."

The preacher's tones were earnest and clear, and as he went on, in language simple and yet saturated with gospel truth, through his sermon, his words fell like the seed of the sower on varied ground.

There was little Mary Bradley, hungering for the bread of life. The sermon, it seemed to her, was for just such poor little, lonely, tried souls as hers. Ready undoubtedly to accept the terms of salvation, she could be seen with her head bowed, eyes closed and lips moving. Good Mrs. Brewer, and other kindred spirits, rejoicing in the truth, silently raised their hearts in prayer that other souls might share the blessedness of pardoned sin. Lucy Day, seeing the clouds of unbelief slowly uplifting in the out-shining of the Sun of Righteousness, was mentally convinced, and so humbled, as she looked back at her own unavailing attempts to find peace without a belief in the Savior's sacrifice. She was almost ready to throw aside all other trust, and renounce all hopes but the hope that clings to the cross alone. Like him of old, she was almost persuaded to be a Christian. God's spirit was at work, and in brokenness of soul she prayed, "Lord, show me the right way."

The afternoon came, and Christ, the humble carpenter of Nazareth, with his daily fulfillment of life's duties, his holy and unblamable walk before God, his lovely and living portraiture of what each Christian soul should strive to do and be was presented. The preacher describing Christ as, the obedient child, the faithful Friend, the patient Teacher, the kind Master, was pictured out as being God, and equal with the Father, and as having "a name which is above every name." At which "every knee should bow, of things in heaven, and things in earth, and things under the earth, and that every tongue should confess that Jesus Christ is Lord, to the glory of God the Father."

Lucy doubted no longer, her only fear now being that she had sinned beyond pardon.

To Mary Bradley a new life had indeed dawned. The child, as she went home across the pastures, and beside the green cornfields, kept saying over and over to herself, "How good God is! How much I will try to love him! How kind everybody is to me! It seems as though everybody and everything are changed, made better and more beautiful than ever before!"

Then, as she sat down to rest a moment under a tree, she thought of her father and his grief for his sin. With this thought came the remembrance of the preacher's words, "Christ for all," and if for all, why not for her father? Her young heart glowed with the desire to see him happy in loving God, and trusting in His salvation. There was comfort in such a hope, and she hastened on to her miserable home, with more of love and compassionate pity for her erring parent than she had ever felt before.

Mr. Bradley was more silent and sad than even he was accustomed to be. In spite of that, he praised Mary's new garments, and called her his "little treasure," and even permitted her to read a chapter from the Bible. Taking the volume himself when she closed, he was seemingly intent on its pages till long after Mary had gone to rest.

Chapter IV
Beginning School Life

shan't play with that beggar child, I do think such folks ought to keep away from a school like ours, where all the first people in the village send their children. I shouldn't think Miss Day would want her here. What are you looking at, Jennie Gleason?"

Blanche Holton had been nurtured in the hot house of pride and fashion, and in the young heart where pity and love should have nestled, scorn and hatred rankled and bore fruit in harsh words and unkind deeds. That Mary Bradley was to attend school was quiet displeasing to her notions of the proper distinctions of society.

"You look like an owl, Jennie Gleason, what are you staring at, I say?"

"Why, I hate to hear you talk so. Mary Bradley isn't a beggar, and she isn't to blame for what her father did, and I think we ought to pity her. I'm sure I do," answered Jennie.

"Well, you can take her as your bosom companion if you wish to," went on Blanche, "but I warn you beforehand, I shan't have anything to do with her nor with you either if you associate with her."

"There comes the teacher," called Susie Bartlett, and the smaller girls started on race to meet her.

"Yes, and there comes the new scholar," sneered Blanche. "Hadn't you better go and meet her, Jennie? I do declare, if she hasn't got on Helen Goldsmith's old pink calico, cut over. I should know that anywhere."

"It looks clean and nice, anyway," said one of the girls.

"And see how pretty her hair curls," said another.

"Pretty, clean and nice!" sneered Blanche.

Anna Green who usually followed in Blanche's wake, added, "I hope her hands are tanned black enough."

While Ella Wood, another of the same clique, said so loud that kind hearted Jennie was almost certain that Mary must have heard, "Carrie Lane wore that old hat two summers ago, and I don't believe it has been even pressed over since."

Mary's face crimsoned, but she smiled pleasantly when Jennie, with a low "for shame," to the thoughtlessly cruel girls, went forward with a half dozen of her companions to meet her. Then Miss Day came, and they all went into the schoolroom.

"May she sit with me?" whispered little Alice Osborne, as she put up her rosy mouth for a good-morning kiss. Lucy smiled back into the loving eyes of the sweet child, and gave the desired permission, and Alice was off like a bird.

"The teacher says you may sit with me," she said in her sweetest tones to the half-frightened child, "and I hope we shall be in the same classes," she went on, "and then we can get our lessons together, and that'll be real nice."

Such a whispering and giggling as there were going on among Blanche Holton, Anna Green and Ella Wood, with a few others who joined them, during the few moments before the bell rang.

Mary Bradley had got up very happy that morning, though she couldn't quite keep back a dread of meeting so many strangers as she knew she must at school, but thought, "God will help me." It cheered her and gave her more courage than all her father's advice, as to being independent and not being put down. If she behaved herself, no one ought to treat her any otherwise than well, for she wasn't to blame for what he had done, or where he had been. He had tried to speak tenderly, but there was yet so much bitterness in the man's heart, born of his remorse and shame, that his tones seemed hard and harsh. However, Mary was beginning to understand her father and she felt that he was doing and saying what he thought was the best for her.

There was more pitiful kindness felt towards him than he was aware of, and more than one Christian heart yearned to do him good. But his repellent manner shut away many from the attempt to win his confidence and help him to a truer view of his own weakness, and of the divine strength upon which he might lean. It angered him that his child should be looked down upon, and he determined if she complained of any neglect or slight shown her, to take her away from school, and do his best to teach her at home.

Alice Osborne's tender and gentle heart was full of love, and her plump little hand kept close hold of Mary' all the while they were reading in the Testament, and through the repetition of the Lord's Prayer. Then before they commenced their lessons, Lucy told them about their sick schoolmate, little Bessie Cudworth. She told them how patient she was, and even happy, because, she said, "God knew what was best for her," and how she had sent her love to the scholars, and hoped they wouldn't any of them get sick. After that, the books were taken out, and study commenced in earnest.

Mary Bradley was not so far behind the other scholars of her own age as might have been expected. She was fond of her books, and had made good use of all the schooling permitted her, and during the lonely months just passed, she had been over and over her books, till she was no unworthy companion for some who looked down on her. To Alice's joy no less than to Mary's, she was placed in the same classes with the former, and with a gratified smile she went busily at work to learn the lessons appointed her.

By and by came the time for recess, and Mary retained her seat thinking she would prefer remaining in to study. But Alice held out her hand, and Jennie Gleason, with one or two others, looked back smilingly, so they went out.

Blanche Holton and her companions went to one side of the playground where they carried on a low-toned conversation, mingled with shouts of laughter and tosses of their heads. Alice led Mary to her favorite seat and produced from her luncheon basket two delicious looking oranges, one of which she offered Mary, with the assertion that she "brought it on purpose."

"You see," she explained, "father got a box of them to carry to Aunt Winnie, who is sick, and he was going to give some to Grandmother, too, and he said I might have six, and so I took two of them today so you could have one.

"Mary's low-spoken "How good you are!" was ample reward to Alice. Then the oranges were cut up and divided, and redivided, till each of the happy group had had a taste. Shortly Jennie proposed that they should sing one of their school songs, so that Mary could learn it. She called to the other girls to come and sing with them, but Blanche answered back scornfully that she preferred to choose her own company, and Anna Green said they might do their own singing.

Just then the bell rang, and the girls all went in. The boys generally were in favor of a cordial befriending of the young stranger, and when, as they frequently had done before, it was proposed to spend the recess in picking and arranging tiny bouquets. Gathered in the woods just across the next field, there was almost a quarrel as to who should make one for Mary Bradley. At last the honor was conferred on Willie Stevens, because they all pitied him, for his only sister had died but a few weeks before. And so it happened that, when the merry group went in with their floral offerings, with the exception of Miss Day's, Mary's nosegay was the prettiest. Then they sang a sweet song about the flowers. Frank Osborne, who had two singing books, one of which he said was "his very own," and the other his "lending book," wrote Mary's name in the latter book, and passed it to his sister to give to Mary. The grateful girl's eyes filled with tears, but she smiled as she took both the flowers and the book, and Willie and Frank felt the happier for their kindness to the little stranger.

Lucy Day was both pained and pleased. She saw more than her pupils were aware of, and the unkind spirit, which a few of them manifested, grieved her much. Still she thought best to take no notice of it, hoping a better feeling would soon overcome the evil then holding sway. At noon many of the scholars went home, and Lucy herself invited Mary to carry her dinner and eat it with her, hoping thus to shield the child from any further suffering that day. Only when they reached Mrs. Brewer's, the good lady, who had been watching them from her doorway, told such a pitiful story of her loneliness, that Mary stayed to bear her company, however Lucy went home alone.

"I've got a granddaughter about your age," said Mrs. Brewer. She had convinced the child that she would be conferring a great favor if she would share the nice dinner so temptingly laid out, "and as I can't see her very often, I wish you would come and see me whenever you can. I loved your mother almost as well as I did my own girls, and I guess she liked me, so I hope we shall be friends."

Mary looked her pleasure and gratitude, and asked presently, "Did you know my Grandmother, too?"

"Yes, dear, we were schoolmates together, and many and many a time have we been to singing schools and quilting parties together, and enjoyed each other's company."

"I wish she was living," said the child, "that is, if it had been for the best."

"That's it, my child, if it could have been for the best God would have let her live, but He knows what is for the best, and so what we can't see plainly we must take on trust. But I'll tell you what you may do, if you like, you may call me Grandma, and I'll love you just as I do my own grandchildren."

"Oh, thank you! I shall like that," said Mary softly, and she kissed the old lady's withered cheek as a seal of the compact.

"I saw you at church, yesterday. Did you enjoy the day?"

Mary looked up at the question. She felt that Mrs. Brewer, who she knew was one of the kind ladies that had furnished her new garments for church and school, could understand her new hopes, and she said earnestly, " 'Twas the happiest day I ever knew. I thought I was happy before I went in the morning! But after I got to church and the minister said so many sweet and good things, I just felt that I could believe God would forgive my sins and accept me, because Jesus died for me, and then when I believed that, I grew happier than ever. The more I thought, the gladder I grew till I wanted to say, 'Praise the Lord!' ever so loud, as I've heard Aunt Molly Gates, at the alms house, say they do at camp meeting. Do you think I was glad because that was God's way letting me know He had forgiven my sins?" she asked looking up into the old lady's beaming face.

"I don't doubt it was, dear child," was her reply, "and do you feel just as happy today?"

"Most of the time," she answered, "only once or twice I've felt a little bit sorry. But it was for something that came before I thought, and the next moment I remembered how much God loved me to give His Son to die for me and everybody else. I tried not to mind little things, and then besides, so many people have been kind to me today, I suppose God told them to be, and I ought to thank Him, hadn't I?"

"Yes, thank Him for everything pleasant, and He'll never fail you," counseled Mrs. Brewer. And then, as Lucy was approaching, she gave the little girl a nice pair of white stockings that she had knit for her, and Mary, with another kiss, said, "Thank you for all your kindness, Grandma," and hastened away to walk with her teacher.

As Blanche and some others of the small minority who turned the cold shoulder to Mary, were kept in for poor lessons, their ill tempers preventing their giving due attention to their tasks, the afternoon recess passed away pleasantly. When school closed at night, Mary said her "good-byes" quickly, and hastened home, anxious to prepare her father's supper before he should return from his work.

This accomplished, she took her favorite seat in the doorway, trying it must be confessed, in rather an unskillful manner, but with patient perseverance, to mend a huge rent in her father's coat. Just as the sun's last rays crept up to the topmost boughs of the tall hemlock across the road, she heard his slow, tired step coming round the corner, and flinging down her work, she ran to meet him. Then she chatted on, telling him everything pleasant she could remember, and as he made an effort to be cheerful and interested, Mary was pleased, and crept up to her little bed truly happy.

Chapter V
Breaking of the Day

"Have you heard the news, Mary?" Alice's voice was very eager, as she met Mary Bradley one morning, when the latter had been attending school about three weeks.

"No," answered the girl, "I don't think I have, at least, no news strange enough to make you look so. What is it?"

"Why, Mr. Holton, Blanche's father, has run away."

"Run away!" echoed Mary, "What for?"

"Oh, he's written other people's names, and got a great deal of money in that way, and so he and his family have lived very finely. But something about a paper that was carried to the Bank made people suspect him. Last night he ran off. They say he left a letter to his wife bidding her 'good-bye,' and telling her she would never see him again. Folks think she will be crazy, she takes on so."

Through all the three weeks Mary had been in the school, Blanche had carried on a constant series of petty unkindness. More than this, she had tried to her utmost, to induce the rest of the scholars to follow her example, and in a few instances had succeeded, so that Mary had felt keenly her cruel scorn. Now came a time that would try Mary's Christian character. Perhaps older people than Mary would have forgotten that vengeance belongeth to God, and way down in their hearts they might have felt glad that the blow had fallen just where it had. God will try the hearts and lives of men, and have said, "Pride goeth before destruction, and a haughty spirit before a fall." But Mary said none of these things, nor do I think the least feeling of gladness entered her heart. The quick tears filled her eyes, and her voice trembled, as she said,

"I'm so sorry, poor Blanche! How badly she will feel! I wish she loved me, so that I could say something to comfort her."

"You dear, darling girl!" exclaimed Alice, pressing her arm closer around her friend. "She's treated you dreadfully, but I knew you would be sorry. Father was sent for this morning, and he said that as many sad scenes as he had been witness to, he never saw one sadder than that at Mr. Holton's. Mrs. Holton was wringing her hands and screaming, 'Oh, my husband, my dear husband!' while Blanche and the younger children were crying around her. The two oldest girls, Etta and Julia, are away at school, and someone has gone for them. Don't it seem so dreadful?"

"Yes, indeed," Mary answered, and when she went into school and saw Blanche's empty seat, she could not keep back her tears of pity, and putting her head down on her desk, she prayed silently that God would comfort the sorrowful family. For Blanche, especially, her sympathy was aroused, for she knew herself how a father's sin casts a shadow over a child's heart and life.

Indeed, the Holtons needed pity. No amount of inquiry brought any further tiding of the guilty man, beyond that of his having taken the night train for New York. What his later movements had been was shrouded in uncertainty. His affairs were in a most ruinous condition, and only the kindness of those whom he had wronged, kept his wife and children from lacking the shelter of a home. As it was, this could only be for a few weeks, while their future was to be provided for.

Mrs. Holton was completely crushed, and taking the two youngest of her children, she went home to her father's, while Etta and Julia, who were really fine scholars, obtained situations, the one as governess, the other as assistant teacher in the school in a neighboring town. Mr. Fernald, Mrs. Holton's father, was far from being a rich man, and in giving his daughter and two of her children a home, he was assuming quite a burden, and so it was decided that Blanche should stay at Martinsville. Mr. Benton, the lawyer's wife, wanted a little girl to help in the care of her children and offered to take Blanche, partly from pity, for the lady knew the child's training had not been such as to render her either willing or efficient.

For two or three days Blanche stayed away from school, and then, as she was so fretful and troublesome at home, her sisters declared she must go while the arrangements were in progress for breaking up the family circle.

The bell had already rung when she entered the schoolroom, and of course, every eye was upon her, some in pity, and some in curiosity. Having been in the habit of putting on so many airs, she had been far from a favorite among the scholars. Yet when she came in, looking so pale and sad, her eyes swollen with weeping, there was not one among the little group but felt sorry for her.

As days went by, however, more than one sorely tried little heart lost patience, and declared she was "more hateful than ever." All Mary's attempts at showing her sympathy were insolently rejected, while her jealous pride, seemingly ever on the watch for neglect, so magnified the slightest deviation from her wishes and opinions, as to render herself, as Frank Osborne told his mother in confidence, "the torment of the school." When she went to Mrs. Benton's that lady kindly permitted her still to attend school, thinking she might the sooner become contented, and knowing with how much interest the approaching examination was anticipated by all the pupils.

Mary Bradley had taken her stand among the best scholars in the school, and there was so much humility in her conduct, even when she most excelled, that only Blanche, and two or three others, felt any envy at her success.

At home Mary assessed her knowledge and strength to make everything as comfortable as possible. Her father, though sad and often very silent, seemed to appreciate her efforts, and was very kind to her. She grew happy and rosy, and went singing about her work through the long, bright mornings. When Mr. Bradley came from his work, in the golden glow of the sunset, he would first hear her sweet, clear tones. Then her happy face, with its dark, truthful eyes and shading of brown curls, would be uplifted for a kiss, as she came bounding out to meet him.

Mary was walking in the light, and her growth in grace had led her where, among the steps of the upward pathway, she found a finger-post with this comforting motto, "Delight thyself also in the Lord, and He shall give thee the desires of thine heart. Commit thy way unto the Lord, trust also in Him, and He shall bring it to pass." So she went on, the one prayer of her heart being that her father might learn the blessed comfort of sins pardoned through a crucified and risen Redeemer, and strong in faith that God would yet grant the fulfillment of this hope. Pastor Adams had returned home, and the minister's words of encouragement strengthened the young disciple in her desires to live near her Saviour and labor in His service.

She had now just passed her eleventh birthday, and gave promise of much strength as well as loveliness of mind and character. She had found many firm friends, who, at first moved by pity, soon found their hearts filled by a warmer feeling toward the lovely child.

Old Mrs. Brewer, or "Grandma," as Mary and indeed half the children in the neighborhood called her, was unsparing in her cheering words and useful directions, giving her lessons in cooking and sewing, and aiding much in making the girl a better house-keeper than many twice her age.

Mr. Bradley was making good wages, and one evening when he went to pay his rent, he was surprised by the proposition that he should buy the place. Instead of paying rent quarterly, as had been agreed upon, pay the same amount if possible as a regular installment towards the amount asked for the house. Enough land was to go with it for a nice garden, and altogether the proposal was so agreeable that the bargain was made on the spot. The gentlemen promised that the requisite papers should be ready in a few days.

A tender spot had been touched in Mr. Bradley's heart. There was more of happiness in his look and tone than he had felt or shown for many a day as he said, "I thank you most sincerely for your kindness, and you shall find your confidence has not been misplaced."

"Oh," said the gentlemen, with a laugh, "I am as much pleased to sell as you are to buy, the place is all running down, and I've been thinking for sometime of making you this offer. The truth is, Bradley," he added more seriously, "you've got more friends here than you are aware of. You did the right thing in coming back here. You've done the right thing, too, in holding yourself aloof from temptation, by staying at home as you have. I've been watching you, and so have others. I haven't been disappointed, you're doing well, and I think you will more than regain your old standing. That little girl of yours is treasure that any man might be proud of, and I hope you'll be happy and prospered in your old age.

Mr. Bradley sat with bowed head. It was very rarely that any one alluded to his past, and never the second time, for the man's face always awed them into silence. But this had been said in such an evident spirit of interest and good feeling, that he could be neither offended nor grieved, only inexpressibly humbled.

"You mustn't spend all the rest of your life mourning over what has gone before," continued the gentleman, as Mr. Bradley still sat silent. "He who died for us on the cross will give you constant comfort, if you will only go to Him. He is ready and willing to save to the uttermost all who come to God by Him. You have been walking in darkness long enough. Why not ask Him to lead you into the light?"

"No, no, there's no comfort for me," Mr. Bradley interrupted him, "all I hope or expect is to make Mary comfortable. God knows I've tried hard to do nothing since I came back here that anybody could find fault with. And I mean to do right, but that won't bring back my wife, or my young manhood's happiness. I thank you for all you've said, but it's useless, I don't see things just as you do, and it won't do any good to talk about it."

Then he went home to tell his good news to Mary, and lay plans for making the house more comfortable. Mary went up to her poor chamber, that her father assured her should soon wear a new aspect, and poured out her thanks to God, from whom she felt that this blessing had come, nor did she forget to add her daily petition that her father might become a Christian. Down in the room below, her father hearing her sweet voice, was moved by some unusual curiosity, listened, and then crept softly up the stairs to her door that no sacred word might be lost.

"Dear Father in Heaven," thus the child pleaded, "bless my dear father, and make him truly thine. He is so unhappy, and only thy love can make him happy. O, teach him the way to the cross, and give him rest. O, help me to be a faithful Christian child, that I may thus recommend my religion to him. May he learn to love thee very soon, if it can be thy holy will, so that he may know how glad and comforted the soul is that loves thee, and trusts in the mercy of thy Son." It seemed as though Mary's heart was so full that she could never stop, but by and by she said, "Now I lay me down to sleep," just as some good old soul had taught her at the almshouse.

Then the man crept down stairs again, with a strange desire that he could feel just as she did, in her trusting faith, tugging strongly at his heartstrings. He got Mary's Bible and read on and on till far into the night, and then as he rose to seek his bed, it seemed that some irresistible feeling moved him to fall upon his knees. All the prayer he offered was, "Lord help me!" However that came from the heart, and went into the ear that is never deaf to the cry of the helpless and grief-laden.

Weeks came and went, and night and morning saw him very busy in making the house more comfortable and even pleasant to the eye. Sometimes he asked Mary to read the Bible to him, and often, very often, when she knew it not, he went softly up the stairs to listen while she prayed. Many were the hours he spent in the study of God's Word, and the prayer, "Lord help me," was not the last he offered. The more he read, the more he prayed, the more plainly his own weakness stood revealed before him. Where he had once gloried in his own strength, and in his power to show to those who knew of his sin and disgrace how he could resist temptation, he now trembled lest he might be left to take some new step astray.

One Sabbath morning he surprised and delighted Mary by appearing in a new suit of clothes and offering to go to church with her. Mary's little room heard a thanksgiving that morning, and her face was fairly radiant with happiness as she came down ready for her walk. The snow lay in unsullied whiteness over the fields, and clung to the pines by the roadside till they looked as though hanging out banners of peace, while over all the blue sky arched cloudless, and the sun shone down in golden splendor.

Mary remembered that summer Sunday, months before, when she thought everything grew in beauty. She had grown into gladness by receiving into her heart Christ's pardon and peace, and she remembered, too, how her life had been blessed since, and her soul seemed ready to burst with its excess of thankfulness. Mr. Bradley was not inclined to talk, but Mary was so happy to have him with her, that she didn't mind his silence, but walked close by his side, her little hand nestled in his, and her face brimful of joy.

Two or three stepped forward to offer a seat, and many Christian souls rejoiced that the wanderer had once more entered the house of God. It lacked but a few days of Christmas, and Mr. Adam's morning discourse was for the children, and was full of beauty, as he told the touching story of Christ's birth and childhood. He told all the wonderful scenes connected wherewith, of the shining of Bethlehem's star, the song of the angels, and the coming of the wise men. Then, he went on with the pure and sorrowful life of the dear Saviour, with all its loving kindness to fallen man, all its pitying tenderness, himself despised and rejected by those whom he came to save. After all his weary wanderings to and fro, forsaken, denied and scorned at the last, he gave up his precious life on the shameful cross, so that all who came to God by him, even the vilest of the vile, could find forgiveness and life eternal. It seemed as though every breath was hushed to listen, while through the solemn stillness the words of the man of God fell like a message from heaven.

There was to be a Christmas celebration of the church and Sabbath school, and when the invitation was given for all to be present, Mary looked up wistfully to meet such a pleasant look on her father's face as gladdened her beyond measure. Thursday evening, the night before Christmas, was looked forward to with much interest, and Mary had been wishing

Breaking of the Day

all along that her father would go, but she had not dared to ask him, now she had a new hope, and was so thankful in the midst of her joy.

This evening was the time for the Sabbath evening services. Mr. Bradley was busy with the Bible and when supper was ready, he asked, as he kissed Mary, and called her his, good little housekeeper, "Would you like to go to the services tonight, Mary?"

The girl looked up in astonishment.

"Oh father, are you going with me?" she asked, her voice quivering, and tears filling her eyes.

"Yes, dear." He spoke playfully, but the next moment father and child were weeping in each other's arms, and Mary's earnest, "Dear father, have you learned to love Jesus?" was answered, "Yes Mary. I've asked Jesus to forgive my sins. And he has. You've got a new father."

"I must pray, father. I must thank the good God for I knew you would love Him, sometime. I have been praying, and I believed my prayers would be answered, but it has all come so sudden."

Such a burst of thanksgiving as went welling up from the grateful heart of little Mary must have been a joy for the angels to hear, and then the father's tremulous tones echoed his daughter's rejoicing words. Who shall say that there was not rejoicing in heaven over this soul newborn into the kingdom? If Mary Bradley was happy in the morning, the evening brought her such an increase of gladness as only the presence and blessing of God can bestow.

A half-hour before the evening service it was the custom for the children, after the opening prayer, to repeat passages of Scripture, in which older people present often, joined them. When it came Mary's turn, her young voice rang out like a bell in the words of Psalm 150, that song of praise in which she felt her own soul could speak out its blessedness. When the verses had been said, and the scholars were again quietly seated, Mr. Bradley arose. With bowed head and clasped hands, testified, "Be it known unto you all, that by the name of Jesus Christ of Nazareth, whom was crucified, whom God raised from the dead, even by him doth this man stand before you whole. Neither is there salvation in any other, for there is no other name under heaven, given among men, whereby we must be saved."

A silence fell over the congregation as Mr. Bradley sat down, and then Mr. Adam's "Let us pray," opened the flood gates of praise and rejoicing, and the evening proved all too short for the pent up feelings that craved utterance.

"Such a happy day," said Mary,

"Such a happy, such a blessed day," said too, her father, while prayers winged their way to heaven, that this token of good might be the forerunner of a copious shower of blessings.

Stephen Bradley had rolled off his burden of guilt and anguish at the foot of the cross, and completely humbled, and feeling his utter helplessness, his cry of "God be merciful to me, a sinner," had received a gracious answer of pardon.

Life looked very different to him now, and though he felt that he could never cease to mourn over the crowning sin of the past, he yet saw comfort in a future devoted to God's service.

Chapter VI
A Christian Home

We go back a few weeks in our story. Lucy Day's school was drawing to a close. For a year she had been at Martinsville, and now the time was nearing when she was again to meet parents and loved ones at home. Her vacations had hitherto been spent with the friends who had procured this situation for her as teacher, and she was looking forward with much interest to the coming pleasure.

Her services had been secured for another year, thus giving her the pleasure of feeling that her efforts were appreciated. She had succeeded in making herself beloved as well as popular, but still she was not satisfied. Her reason convinced, her heart still remained under the thrall of a proud unwillingness to trust herself and her salvation to Jesus alone. She was still anxious to win peace in her own way, through the patient endurance of trials, through kind deeds, and through loving self-denials. In short, in any and every way that held out a prospect of obtaining favor with God, and securing her a good hope of a home in Heaven. No such favor seemed to smile upon her; no such hope gave her peace and comfort. Pastor Adams, who, at the time of her receiving the note from him, had been in the place but a few months, had become a personal friend, and often, very often, presented the theme of the cross to her faithfully, and ever found an attentive listener.

Little Bessie Cudworth had died rejoicing in her Savior's presence, and leaving as a parting legacy to her beloved teacher, the fondly expressed hope that she should meet her in Heaven. Mrs. Brewer grew more and more anxious, as time went on, that her young friend should know, by personal experience, the joys of a living faith in the Redeemer. Like the young man in the days when our Saviour trod the earth, she was all that was lovely and amiable in disposition and daily life, but, like him, she lacked "the one thing needful."

They were trimming the schoolroom with wreaths and flowers the night before final exams, and Lucy had just fastened a beautiful evergreen cross against the wall, with the letters, "I.H.S." underneath, when Mary Bradley, coming in with a fresh supply of floral treasures asked in her gently way,

"Teacher, what does that mean?"

"It stands for a Latin sentence, which means 'Jesus, Saviour of man,'" answered Lucy, "or at least that is one meaning attached to it, sometimes it is said to stand for other sentences."

"But that must be the sweetest, don't you think so teacher?" queried the child.

"Yes," answered Lucy, "I like that rendering very much but, Mary, do you know the meaning of a circle?"

Mary did not know, but Alice Osborne did.

"Mother told me the other day," she said, "when Father and she were talking about some of the emblems in the new church, which they went to see, the last time they visited the city. She said a circle was an emblem of eternity, because it is endless, and there was another figure, a three-sided one, that indicated the trinity, and she told me what you just told Mary about those letters, too. I like that the best."

"'Jesus, Saviour of man!' I wonder any one can ever forget that," said Mary softly. "I'm so much happier since I knew about Jesus. When I lived at the almshouse, there were two or three poor old ladies there all the time since I can remember, three at first, and then one died, and they were just as happy as could be, though one was blind and the other two couldn't walk a step."

"Were they all the old ladies there were in the house?" asked Alice.

"Oh, no, there were lots of others," Mary continued, "but these were

A Christian Home

in a room together, and when I got big enough, I used to stay in their room ever so much to wait upon them, be, 'eyes and feet for them,' they used to say."

"Did you say that they were always happy?" Lucy was getting interested. Blind, lame and in an almshouse, and yet always happy! If only she could learn their secret!

"Yes, they were just the darlingest old ladies you ever saw, and I was going to tell you they were always talking about Jesus and Heaven, and I liked to hear them, and they wanted me to be good. One of them, Aunt Winnie Gray, taught me to say, 'Now I lay me down to sleep,' and made me promise I would say it every single night. She said she always said it just as her mother told her to when she was a little girl."

"Why, I thought that was for children to say, not for old folks," said Frank Osborne, who, with several others, had joined the circle.

"No," said Alice positively, "it's just as good for old folks. Father told me the other night that he always said it when he went to bed. Then I went and asked Grandma, and she said she did, too."

"Tell some more, Mary," urged one of the girls.

"I wasn't going to say much more," said Mary, "only that I think 'twas because they loved Jesus so well that they were so happy. I used to wish I knew all about Jesus, and how to please him, and that I might love him, so that I could be happy like them."

"Happy in a poorhouse! They must have been jolly old girls," interrupted Frank, who, like many other boys, thought it smart to mix in a little spice of slang with his conversation.

"For shame, Frank! Father wouldn't let you talk so, that isn't a proper way to speak of the good old ladies."

Alice was in earnest, and Frank, who really intended no disrespect said, "I'll take it all back, little sister, most likely they were good old salts of the earth."

"I don't think that mends the matter much," said Lucy, when the laugh had subsided, "it isn't exactly respectful for you to speak so."

Mary looked grieved and Alice said softly, her loving little heart pained that her brother should grieve her friend, "Frank doesn't mean half so bad as it sounds, but I wish he wouldn't talk so."

"I won't any more." Frank looked his sincerity and Mary was entreated to tell some more.

"When Aunt Winnie died, she had been lame for a long time," proceeded Mary, "she told me to be sure and never forget that none but Jesus could make people happy when they come to die. I used to think about it ever so much."

Just then Mary caught a glimpse of Blanche Holton's scornful face, and heard her low spoken remark, "Just as though I should have cared what those old paupers said, besides, I should be ashamed to own that I ever lived in such a place."

The child stopped, her fair face flushed with suppressed feeling, and Lucy who had both seen the look and heard the cruel words, spoke more sternly than they ever remembered to have heard her before, "Blanche, never allow me to hear you speak like that again. No one need feel ashamed of anything but sin, and it is no sin to be poor, or even to live at an almshouse."

Blanche was silenced, but sat twining her wreath with a face dark with passion. By and by Alice asked,

"Did you learn to love Jesus at the almshouse, Mary?"

"I loved Him some," Mary answered, "but I used to feel that I was so wicked, he couldn't love me. So I went on, sometimes real glad, and sometimes just as sorry till after I came here. Then I thought about it more and more. Pastor Adams used to talk to me, and then that first Sunday I went to church here, when that new minister preached who was here while Pastor Adams was gone away, I understood how Jesus could save us better than ever before, and it's been all plain ever since. I want to do all I can to please and honor Jesus, but still I know that won't save me. He's done that great work for me, and I've go to believe, and leave all the rest with Him."

"But supposing you are mistaken?"

Mary looked up surprised that her teacher should ask such a question.

A Christian Home

"But I can't be," she answered, "the Bible makes it all so plain."

"But supposing you are," persisted Lucy, "what then?"

"Why, I should have to leave it all with God, there would be no other way, and He never does wrong."

"Dear child," whispered the teacher, "I wish I had your faith."

Mary looked wistfully into the young lady's face, who had moved away to answer some question relative to the trimming, and she thought, "I'll ask God to give her faith."

It seemed to Lucy that every conversation on religious topics in which she became engaged, drifted into the one theme, Christ and His power to save, and she wished she might either wholly believe, or else that her doubts might be strengthened to a certainty.

Two days later and she was on her journey home. Her school finished to the satisfaction of all parties, bearing with her the remembrance of Mary's parting words, "Dear teacher, I love you, and you don't know how much I want you to love Jesus, I'm praying God to give you faith."

Soon after Lucy left to assume her teacher duties at Martinsville, the Day family had moved from their village home into the old farmhouse, where Mr. Day's boyhood had been spent. This place being the only portion of his large amount of property that he felt at liberty to retain, the rest had all passed into other hands. Lucy had dreaded going by her fondly loved home, and finding the family in a new abode, for, though the old homestead had seemed pleasant as the home of Grandpa and Grandma, it was dreadfully old fashioned, and out of the way.

It was a clear, bright evening in early August, when after a long day's ride in the cars, Lucy stepped out on the platform of the station nearest her home. A stout, sun-browned young man stood eagerly watching the alighting passengers, so much had he change from the delicate student of a year ago, that she failed to recognize him, until he sprang forward with a glad,

"Here you are at last Lucy, I feared I was to be disappointed tonight."

"And how are they all at home?" she asked, when the first bustle of starting had subsided, and they were speeding toward home.

"All well, Grandma has been a little ailing, but she's better, and the children have been planning any number of nice times when you should come."

"And Father and Mother, are they happy, and do they have to work hard?"

"Happy as clams at high water, and as for work, we all work, there isn't a drone in the whole hive. Father thinks that if we are prospered I shall be able to go on with my studies in a year or two. I mean to enter college, for I study now, and last week the committee offered me the school in the Hill District, so I'm going to turn pedagogue this coming winter, if I'm prospered."

"And Susan?" queried Lucy.

"Oh, she's dress maker in general for our own family, and the whole neighborhood, but Lottie is the jolliest of all. Grandpa says she is a very sunbeam he ever saw. There's no crying for the old place. Father says this last year has been the best he has ever known. There's been a new church formed over at the village. We all have become members, and Lucy," the young man's voice faltered with earnest feeling, "the love of Jesus is worth more than the world can give or take away. I hope, if God spares my life, to devote it to His service. I mean to be a minister."

"What's become of your ambition? I thought you used to say you should take 'Excelsus' for your motto, and that you meant to scale the very pinnacle of fame."

"'Excelsus' will do for a motto now, dear sister, and with more truth than ever. I do indeed want to go 'higher, still higher,' till I stand at last on the Heavenly mountains, and as for my ambition, I've laid it at the foot of the cross."

"Why haven't some of you written about all this?"

"Hasn't Susan written?"

"She has mentioned the new church several times, and the pleasant meetings, but I supposed you only went there because it was nearer, or the minister was smarter, or something of the kind."

"I heard Lottie talking about writing the other day, and she said you

A Christian Home 47

used to say that people who believe as we do, were fanatical and set in their opinions. She knew you were coming home soon, you had better see how happy religion made us, not hear and be prejudiced before you reached home. John and I agreed with her, but Susan wanted to write, and I supposed she did. It was only at last communion, a fortnight ago, that we united with the church and you never saw anybody so happy as Grandpa and Grandma were. Grandpa said he felt that he could say like Simeon of old, 'Lord, now lettest thou thy servant depart in peace, according to thy word, for mine eyes have seen thy salvation.' I think the little ones are very thoughtful, Anna, especially. She and Willie have both changed wonderfully during the past year."

"All but me," said Lucy, as though thinking aloud.

"There's room for you," said her brother tenderly.

Presently, from a rock by the roadside, two children sprang up at their approach, with shouts of, "Is it really you, Lucy?" and, "I told you we should come and meet you, Fred," and then the two, a boy and a girl, clambered into the wagon, and the party went on again.

"There's John and the girls at the gate," was presently announced, and Lucy hardly knew whether to laugh or cry, for such a tumult of joyful excitement followed her arrival. In the great old-fashioned kitchen the lights gleamed over a cheerful looking tea table. The simple, but bountiful repast, rendered still more inviting by its adorning of flowers and the purple and crimson of the pyramids of berries, crowned with snowy peaks of sugar. On Lucy's plate was a simple drawing, Anna's last effort. Above the door was written with love, "Welcome home!" Anna had been working over it for weeks and everything about it, even the curling tendrils of the vine that drooped around and above. Decorations had been touched and retouched, till, in the light of home affection, it looked just what Lucy pronounced it, "A perfect little gem."

As they grouped around the table, a hush fell on the merry band, while with bowed head Mr. Day returned thanks for that night's blessings, and craved a continuance.

How strange it seemed to Lucy, and then the after supper gathering around the family altar, when a chapter was read, a hymn sung, and a prayer offered, ending, as the thanks at the table had done, with "for Jesus sake." She somehow felt like one shut out. Here was a tangible peace that she did not possess. But why couldn't she as well as they? This was such a different coming home from what she had looked forward to. She knew Mary and Lottie had written very cheerful letters, and she remembered now how many times they had mentioned God's goodness to them. She had somehow got the idea they were following her lead, and were trying to perfect their own characters, and gain the Christian's hope and gladness by their own unaided efforts. So, while her own way seemed to grow more and more hedged up, she had written long letters to them encouraging them in their efforts. Thinking thus, she rather expected to find them weary amid their seeking, and inclined to murmur at their fate. Only here was no murmuring, instead of it, there seemed an evident desire to count their blessings, and view them as the gift and token of a Father's love. Happy as their old home had been, this was happier in a fuller sense than that had ever proved.

"We have gained wealth higher than any we have lost, my daughter," said her father, as Lucy lingered in saying her "good-nights."

"It's so strange no one wrote me of this directly, could you once think I should fail of being interested?"

"Oh, no indeed! Darling Lucy," it was Lottie who spoke now. "But we knew you felt so differently, and then we agreed to pray for you, and somehow it seemed that praying might do more good than writing, though it did seem like shutting you out from our joy not to write you all about it. I did allude to the change in my feelings, but you took both Mary's letters and mine so differently from what we meant, that we prayed all the more for you, and for ourselves, too, that we might live our religion, and thus make you like, and, we hoped, share it with us."

"I can bear this no longer." Lucy broke down in sobs and with her head in her mother's lap, wept convulsively.

"Is it because you think we haven't shown confidence in you, dear sister?' whispered Susan, kneeling beside her.

"No, no, no," sobbed Lucy, while her tears flowed afresh, "but I've been fighting against your prayers, against the Saviour, all summer. I have tried to harden my heart against the truth that through Him must come our salvation, and I've been trying to save myself. The more I tried the more unhappy I grew, and everything seemed to conspire against my assumed belief, and the more I clung to it, the weaker it showed itself to be.

"That is what we all find, my child, when we lean on broken staves of our own forming," said Mr. Day, while John added,

"I've walked over the same quicksand, Lucy, I tried hard enough to save myself, but I had to give up. I forced myself to do a great many unpleasant things, because I thought there would be some merit in them, and I tried to hunt up ways to make myself a name for goodness, as well as to find favor with God, but 'twas all in vain. There is only one way to be saved, and that is by Christ, and if we really love Him what we once forced ourselves to do as a duty, often loses its unpleasantness, and becomes, for Him, a labor of love. You will find it so, precious sister."

Lucy's first night at home was a sleepless one. She thought of her hopes, her aims, her rejection of Christ, and of His long suffering patience, and it seemed to her she had never felt so guilty, so utterly hopeless and helpless before.

Just as the morning dawned, like an angel's whisper, so it seemed to her, came the thought, "He saves others, He will save me, for He saves to the uttermost all who go to God by Him." Then she crept softly out of bed, and falling on her knees, prayed as she had never prayed before. The burden of her prayer was, "O Lord, save me, the chief of sinners, for Christ's sake, I give myself to Thee, 'tis all I can do, help me to trust in Jesus alone, and in him find peace and pardon." Such a fullness of joy and trust flooded her that, for a moment, she could only bow in silent rapture. Her burden was all gone, she felt like a new being, and springing from the floor, she met Lottie's questioning look with the glad answer,

"I'm not alone any longer. He's my Saviour, too! Oh, I never knew what happiness was before," and then in the gray and gold of the dawning, Susan came in to rejoice with them. Anna soon followed, and the four sisters, one in heart, knelt in prayer together. Anna had whispered, "Now what a happy family we shall be!"

A happy family indeed, happy in the Lord, and their oneness of interest in His saving mercy.

Grandpa Day's heart was so full that he broke down in the midst of his prayer. Mr. Day's was like a song of praise, and when they rose from their knees, without a spoken word, as with one accord, they broke forth into the triumphant strains of "Praise God from whom all blessing flow."

Truly Lucy had found an open door, and her "welcome home" had been sweeter than any artist's brightest colors could have painted it. In the midst of her joy she could not rest till she had stolen away alone for a little while, and penned a few loving lines to little Mary Bradley, that she knew would send a thrill of gladness to the hearts of her many Christian friends at Martinsville.

Chapter VII
Joy in Labor for Others

The Saturday afternoon when Mary Bradley received her teacher's letter, was one of those days of September, when the sunlight lies in great, golden patches on green pastures, the waving corn-fields, and the brown stubble where the grain nodded. And when the shadows chase each other hither and thither, while the purple of distant mountains and the blue of the sky is over spread by that wonderful haze that make the far-off appear a tangible presence.

Mary wanted to do more than, just at that time, she could see herself able to accomplish. She was only a poor little girl, and from the little she could earn picking berries, she could spare but a mite for each of the various charities in which she was just now interested. It was something new to the child, the luxury of giving, and she had anxiously waited for the berries to ripen, that she might not only help herself, but aid others also.

In her talks with Grandma Brewer, the good lady had told her that little deeds of kindness, if done in Jesus' name and for Jesus' sake, were charity as really as the gift of silver and gold. She repeated the Savior's words, "For I was an hungered and ye gave me meat, I was thirsty, and ye gave me drink, I was a stranger, and ye took me in, naked, and ye clothed me, I was sick, and ye visited me, I was in prison, and ye came unto me." Thus telling her of a variety of ways in which Christ might be served through His disciples.

So, in addition to her forenoon's work, Mary had picked a few quarts of nice berries. In the afternoon she went on a long walk through the forest paths and down by the sunny meadow, to the home of a poor cripple. Who, had united to a man more crippled in soul than she was in body, lived a sad and lonely life, often seeing no one but her husband for days together.

As she went along, Mary gathered here and there bright-hued wild flowers, till she had as lovely a bouquet as one might desire.

She found the invalid more than usually ailing, but glad and thankful to see her. Quick and gently in her movements, the little girl, intent on her purpose of doing something for somebody, soon had the disorderly room in a better state. She bathed the sufferer's face and hands, arranged her bed more comfortably, and then, after nicely combing her hair, brought some of the great, luscious blackberries, that the woman declared did her good even to smell. The flowers too, received a hearty welcome, and then Mary sat down for a chat before going home.

"Don't you get lonely?" she asked in her gentle, sympathizing way, that unconsciously carried comfort with it.

"I'm most always lonely," replied the woman, "I suppose everybody and everything is made for some purpose but I often wonder what I am made for. I certainly can't do anybody any good. Here I lie from morning till night, nothing but a burden."

"You've done me good this very afternoon," said Mary.

Mrs. Staple, for that was the woman's name, looked up astonished.

"I don't see how," she said.

"Why, it's just this way," said Mary, "I've made myself really unhappy lately because I couldn't do everything I wanted to do. I wanted to give when I hadn't the money to give, and I'm afraid I showed a very naughty spirit. However seeing you lying here made me think that most likely God has different ways for us to show our love to Him, you by just being patient, and I by doing all I can do, but not making myself unhappy about what I can't do. And then, besides,"

Mary hesitated, but Mrs. Staples' "What else, dear? It does me good to hear you talk," gave her courage, and she went on:

"Then when I saw you so lame, I thought how thankful I ought to be that I can walk about, I don't know as I ever thought to thank God for that before, but I won't forget it again."

"You're a precious child," said the woman, her eyes filling with tears. "I wish it could have been right for my girls to live, but they both died when they were babies. Sometimes I've felt thankful they are safe with God in Heaven, they would have had such a hard lot in life if they had lived."

"Doesn't Pastor Adams ever call to see you?"

Mary was sorry that she had asked the question, for the swift tears and quivering lips told her that she had unwittingly touched a tender spot.

"He had tried twice to see me, but James had been drinking both times, and the last time, he got so angry at something the minister said, that he swore he would shoot him if he ever darkened his doors again. I was so frightened I got Dr. Osborne to tell Pastor Adams, for if James wasn't just right, he would as willing shoot as not. He says he don't want any priest whining round him, and what's more, he won't have any. I would give almost anything to see the minister, but unless he knew just when James was away, it wouldn't be safe for him to come."

"Is he always cross?" It seemed a delicate question to Mary, but her feeling of interest in the poor woman prompted it.

"Oh, no, not always, sometimes he is very kind. He has never refused to let me see the doctor, but once in a while he gets in a perfect fury, and will hide my Bible and threaten to destroy it, and perhaps go off and leave me all day alone, but it's not so with him very often."

Mary had cheered and gladdened a lonely heart, and had thus been herself cheered, and she bounded off towards home with a light step. Just before she reached it she met Alice Osborne, whose first greeting was,

"Which hand will you have, right or left?"

"The right," and then a letter was produced for "Miss Mary Bradley."

A quick flush mounted to Mary's temples, as she took the letter.

"I never had a real letter, with a stamp on it, before, in my whole life," she said.

"Let's sit down here under the maples and read it, don't you see it is from Miss Day? I know her writing whenever I see it."

Alice seemed to feel that she held a joint claim with Mary on the letter, and Mary had not a thought of disputing her, so the precious letter was opened and read.

"My Dear Little Mary," so it commenced, "Your prayer is answered. God has given me faith to believe, and now I feel that my sins are washed away in the blood of Christ, and peace like a river gladdens my soul. I can understand your happiness now, and share it, too, and I hope when I go back to Martinsville, if God spares my life, to live more for His glory, and be a more faithful teacher than I have ever been before.

"God has poured out His spirit in our family, and we are all one in Christ. You must tell Grandma Brewer how happy I am, and give love to her, and Alice, and all the friends I love so well. Can't you and Alice, and some of the other girls, write to me? I will answer all your letters. You mustn't leave off praying for me, Mary, for I'm only a learner in the school of Christ, and need constant help." And then with fond "good-byes," and an abundance of good wishes, the letter ended.

"Oh, isn't that good?" exclaimed Alice, but Mary only laid her face down on the letter that had brought her such glad news, and cried in very joyfulness, while she thanked God silently.

Presently Alice's, "I've come to stay to supper with you, Mary," aroused her to a sense of her inhospitality, and she answered, quickly,

"I'm ever so glad. I've got some of the nicest blackberries you ever saw."

"Mother said we could play picnic," went on Alice, "and she made me a plateful of delicious little pies. Mrs. Brewer happened to come in and found I was coming, and so when I came by there she stopped me, and sent you the dearest little loaf of plum-cake, all covered with frosting, and half a dozen early pears. Father's coming by here this evening, and he said I could stay if I wished to do so, till he called for me."

The shadows lay long on the clover-dotted yard, and the two girls went in to get the supper ready before Mr. Bradley should get home.

"We'll wait for him," Alice proposed, for 'twill be so much nicer, and Father won't come after me this long time."

Alice loved Mary very dearly, and somehow the merry little girl had, in her previous calls at Mary's home, so won upon the sad and weary heart of her father, to make her welcome certain. Trained in a Christian home, she was fearless in her loving pity, hearing daily prayers that offered that the sinful and the sorrowful might be reclaimed and comforted. She had no other feeling for the stern, silent man than a most tender compassion. So, from the very morning when, spying him in the street, Alice had run after him to send a message to Mary, her sweet, trusting eyes upraised confidently to his, he had taken her into his affection.

"We'll have a clean tablecloth tonight," Mary said, as Alice drew out the table, when the fire was burning brightly in the stove, and the teakettle had been filled with fresh water, "and we've got some new white dishes. Father brought them home last night. He says we'll get things by degrees, and after a while we shall have things as nice as anybody needs. You know this is our house now, don't you?"

"Yes," said Alice, "and I'm real glad, and Father says he is, too."

"I had splendid luck in making bread today." Mary opened her cupboard with such a house-wifely air of importance as would have been amusing to other eyes than the partial ones of her little friend, who thought Mary and all her doings perfection itself. She went on thus,

"Grandma Brewer told me just how to do it, and it's just as light as a sponge. It's so much better than having baker's bread, as we did at first. Oh, we did live dreadfully for a while. I didn't know anything about cooking, nor Father either, and such messes as we did fix up! I used to wish myself back at the almshouse ever so often."

"You don't now, do you?" Alice asked, as she looked up eagerly, while busily picking over some of Mary's berries into a pretty white dish.

"No, indeed, I'm learning how to do lots of things, and growing bigger every day. There! The water boils, now I'll put some tea down for Father. I like flowers on the table don't you, Alice? When you get the berries done, we'll run down the road and get some maiden's bower, some wild asters, and with some of my sweet peas, that'll be a nice bouquet, I think Father likes them."

"So does my father," said Alice, as she went to wash her hands. "Why, Mary! How bright your wash dish is."

"Yes," Mary laughed as she answered, "Father told me, when he saw it last night, that 'twould be quite a saving of looking-glass. I did it yesterday. I got some sand down by the river, and I made things shine at a great rate. I was tired, I tell you, but they looked enough better to pay for all that."

"Don't the table look beautiful? Good enough for a queen!" Alice clapped her dimpled hands with childish glee, "You're real splendid, Mary, and Mother says it's wonderful how a little girl like you can do so much. I'm just as much astonished as she is."

"Why, I just keep doing, that's all, and when I get tired I make believe it's play, and that I'm only doing it for fun. Then the work goes easy, and when that don't do, why, I think of what Grandma Brewer says, that work done well is work done for God, and little duties faithfully attended to, help to make us ready for bigger ones. There comes Father, won't he be surprised?"

The man came wearily in and such a pretty picture met his gaze, as many a richer home would have failed to display. The room was bright with the golden glow of the sunset, the singing of the kettle on the stove, the perfect neatness of everything, the table with its new white ware and nice looking food, the pears, berries and flowers. Still, prettier than all, the two little girls, with their happy greetings. These were some of the golden links of the chain that, in God's providence, was drawing the stricken man away from the mire of his sins, into the path where faith and hope in God lead the pilgrims who go to Him for guidance, and giving him a new and higher life.

"You've got two house-keepers now," said Alice, gaily.

Mary asked, "Are you tired tonight, Father?"

Then they bustled about to put up the chairs, and bring the tea from the stove, while Mr. Bradley assured Alice that he was glad his family was growing larger, and declared himself rested since he came into the house. They sat down to supper, and by and by, Mary had to get a lamp as they lingered so long at the table, and they had but just got the dishes nicely washed and put away, when the doctor called for his little girl, and the happy visit ended. Mary had tried to make others happy that day, and she had found, as such workers always find, that the joy, which she craved for others, was returned to her in unexpected measure.

She was not quite certain of her father's sympathy in her gladness over her letter, but Alice had mentioned it. So she brought it to him for his perusal, and she thought there were tears in his eyes when he gave it back to her with a good night kiss.

Mary went early to church the next morning that she might stop and tell her good news to Grandma Brewer. Just as they were leaving Grandma's gate, Pastor Adams paused to speak to them. When she told him, too, the good man went into his pulpit rejoicing anew at the wonderful power of the gospel, and the blessedness with which a saving knowledge of it fills the soul.

Chapter VIII
Temptation and Triumph

Lucy's vacation was nearly over, and she had not seen Laura Howard, the latter being absent on a journey among the mountains with a party of friends. One night, however, Fred came home from the village with the news of her return, adding,

"She and Harry are coming over this evening, and, Lucy, you must expect to see a change in them both, in Harry, especially."

Before she could ask an explanation, the noise of wheels announced their approach, and Lucy hastened to the door to receive her friends.

Laura Howard was beautiful, and with ample means at her command had a refined taste in matters of dress. For several months after Lucy's departure from home, a regular correspondence had been maintained between the two girls, but as time went on, Laura grew remiss in writing, and for some weeks before Lucy came home, no letters had been received from her. Dress, and the light frivolities of fashionable life had been the prevailing topics of Laura's letters, and Lucy, whose recent life had been so different, and fraught with so much anxious and earnest thought, was often pained at her lack of what seemed true and noble feeling.

From earliest childhood, the two had been on terms of the closest intimacy, and if Lucy had not had other anxieties of more vital importance, it would have been a sore trial to her affectionate heart to feel that her friend was forgetting her. Often since her return home she had thought of Laura. Her wish had found quick entrance within her heart, that the friend who had shared her childhood's joys and griefs, might be a sharer with her in this new joy, this blessedness above all that earth can give, and that earth can never take away.

There was certainly no lack of affection in Laura's return of Lucy's warm greeting, and for a little time Lucy thought her brother was mistaken in regard to the change in her friend. Laura had been visiting some of the most beautiful of the mountainous portions of New England, but her conversation failed to show that her pictures of memory had received many additional treasures from the scenes of beauty and grandeur on which her gaze had fallen.

"And you visited Echo Lake?" asked Lottie.

"Yes, I went there one moonlight evening," was the answer, "but I wasn't particularly pleased, the echoes are well enough, but not worth making so much fuss over."

"Shall I throw light on Laura's indifference to the wonders of Echo Lake? The truth was, Miss Sallie Clinton, the prospective heiress of half a million, was glorifying the region about that time, and all Laura's best and most eligible beaux were off duty, chiefly, it must be confessed, on Miss Clinton's account."

Laura's look, and her, "For shame, Harry, how can you tell such a tale?" were both sufficiently fraught with scorn to show that her brother had touched upon an unpleasant theme, while he went on, his handsome lip curling in a smile that was half a sneer,

"'Tis true, young ladies, true as the gospel, and I believe the bewitching Miss Sallie knew it, too! She did her prettiest to craze both beaux and belles, the first with admiration, the latter with envy, and Laura was no more proof against this feminine weakness than the rest."

"You talk like a fool tonight," retorted Laura, "and you acted like one that night. You were all like a set of millers buzzing and fluttering round a candle, they must all get their wings singed before they are satisfied, and 'twas just so with you. Sallie Clinton didn't care a straw about one of you, but you couldn't see the truth till you got the wings of your self conceit singed a little, and not a very little, either."

"The wound festers yet," laughed the imperturbable Harry, and then

Lucy, anxious to change the subject, asked,

"Did you like what you met at Newport or Saratoga best?"

"Oh, Newport, by all odds, " Laura answered, "I never saw so much style in my life before. Some of the first people in the land were there. There were hops every night, and the dancing was heavenly, I never knew what real enjoyment was till I went there. One evening there was worth a dozen Echo Lakes, with all the rest of the so much fussed about mountain scenery thrown in."

"What hard work it must have been to use up all the adjectives in the language, as you did, if you found the mountains as dull as you pretend." Harry seemed to be in a peculiarly provoking mood.

Laura prefixed her description of the pleasure of Newport with, "If I possessed a memory as tenacious of trifles as yours is, I should consider it no blessing, of course one has to pretend to some admiration, or else be out of fashion."

"And one had better be out of the world than submit to such a terrible fate." Harry laughed maliciously, while his sister, turning away from him, went on,

"Such magnificent turnouts as one saw on the drives, they quite put me out of patience with common carriages, and the gold and silver on some of the harnesses were worth a small fortune. Then there were parties for horseback riding almost every day, and Cousin Bettie Danforth and I wore off the palm for fine riding, so they all said. Uncle Danforth hired two of the finest horses in Newport for us, for the season, and we had new suits, that everybody said were vastly becoming. At Saratoga there was,"

"Let me help you." Harry spoke mockingly. "There were fuss, flummery and fashion, show, diamonds and dancing, envy, emptiness and elegance, and, crowning all this, the most magnificent flirting I ever saw, or ever desire to see. Laura took to it royally as to the manor born. I was proud of her, I assure you, Lucy. 'Twas better than the opera, star singers and all. I wonder who flirted the most."

Laura was fast losing her patience, and Mary, who was pained at the evident lack of sympathy between the brother and sister, proposed that Laura should take a seat at the piano, while the rest sang. Now came a new difficulty. Laura could play only the newest and most fashionable music. While the self-helping, active life of the young Days had wrought out a kindred strength and pure earnestness of feeling, that sought some nobler expression than the frivolous words that were fitted into the fashionable opera music in which Laura delighted. Many of her songs they had never even heard of, while their favorite ballads, and really fine collection, she pronounced "out of style," and "old-fashioned."

"Screeching is all the rage, now a days," said Harry, "so everybody who is anxious to be thought anybody, must learn to screech, nothing else goes down with the beau monde."

Hence through the whole evening, every effort to lead the conversation into higher channels failed of success. Harry Howard's handsome face bore the too certain marks of habitual evil, while his boyish love of fun seemed to have grown into a cynical contempt of life, and of all who shared life with him. His two years at college had been a curse instead of a blessing. Fred Day, in his new insight into a nobler state of living, felt that the misfortune which had sent him home from collegiate halls in the first year of his course, was a blessing whose disguise was fast dropping off. Manhood was felt to be far more valuable than a mere diploma. Prosperity had marred the spiritual, while it had seemingly enlarged and glorified the worldly prospects of the Howards, and only the grace of God could save them from making an utter failure of life.

Just as they were leaving, Harry turned toward Lucy with the query, "Have you and Laura made any arrangement for that reunion of confidences, that comparison of the past year's items of interest. I believe it was to come off when you two met again under those fine old trees where I turned eavesdropper a year ago? I am at your service any day."

"I don't think we've mentioned the place tonight," said Laura, "but I would like to go if Lucy chooses."

"That's my mind, exactly," continued Harry. "I want to be present at the interview. I am anxious to know if all Lucy's plans for self-control and self-poise, and a never failing purpose to read down difficulties have proved as easy of accomplishment as they looked feasible in theory. Did you know what a heroine, what 'a perfect woman, nobly planned,' your sister was to be, in her life at Martinsville?" he asked, turning to John, whose fond eyes were bent upon Lucy's downcast face.

"No, I never heard her plans as to any extra heroism," John answered, "but," he added more solemnly, and with a loving pressure of his sister's hand, "I do know that her aims are now to venture into no broader sphere of action than she can walk in. With one hand clinging to the cross of Christ, where she hopes to find both guidance and salvation."

A light reply seemed trembling on Harry's lips, but something kept back its utterance, and the two soon made their adieus and departed.

"There is the wreck of a noble nature," said Fred

While Lucy added, "I hardly know which is most to be pitied, Harry's scornful mockery of life's best feelings equally with its most foolish foibles, or Laura's utter giving up to fashion and her rules."

"Mr. Howard has been wonderfully prospered in his business," remarked Mr. Day, who came in at the moment Lucy was speaking, "but from all I can learn, both parents and children are going down hill morally and spiritually. Howard and I have been friends all our lives, and commenced business at about the same time. Lately he has avoided me, and has used all his influence against the building of the new church, and the gathering in of outsiders to hear the gospel preached."

"Was he always so bitter?"

Mrs. Day looked up at Mary's question, for she well remembered the time, in years gone by, when the now fashionable Mrs. Howard was simply sweet Agnes Dana. "Before the Howards got married," Mrs. Day said, "he said he never had much respect for religion," then she added gently, "I knew then, even in my worldliness, that Agnes was linking her fate with one who would never ennoble her character and lift her aspirations. She was of a gently, clinging nature, and gave herself up to his guidance, and in the end has proved herself an adept in fashionable folly. Dear husband," Mrs. Day looked in the direction of her husband, a tear dropped off her cheek, "a year ago I envied Agnes Howard her husband's property, now I thank God for the misfortune that has led us to Him. Things that a year ago seemed a trial and a penance, now seem precious privileges, and to see our children, one by one, seeking the ark of refuge, is joy too great for expression. I can never be thankful enough, and all the fine surroundings of our old home seem, in my memory, dearly as I prized that home, as dross when compared with the peaceful calm that seems to hallow the very air we breathe here."

"Amen, and amen, dear wife," said her husband, and Lottie, turning to the piano, began playing "Sweet Home," in the singing of which the rest united, and then they parted for the night.

Lucy felt deeply the change in her friend, which was the more marked in contrast with her own new found hopes and aims, which led her in one direction while Laura went another. During the past twelve months Lucy had been wandering in darkness, but ever with a desire to get into the narrow way that must be trod by all who would reach heaven, but she had lately entered by the only door, the door o'er shadowed by the cross of Christ. Laura, turning deliberately into the broad way, was still feeding her immortal soul with the husks of this world's pleasures, and asking nothing better. There was only one place where Lucy felt that the burden of her desires for her friend could be laid down, and that was at the foot of the cross, where hope and consolation and peace are never sought in vain.

Harry Howard and his sister rode home in the quiet hush of night. The soft gleam of moonlight gilding the shadows of the way would make them eloquent to hearts, which hear God's still, small voice. In the calm of the nighttime, the joyful awakening of the morning, the radiant brightness of noon day, and the purple, crimson and amber of the sunset, found the two hearts illy fitted to enjoy the beauty around. Laura was disappointed in Lucy.

"I'm provoked," she exclaimed, pettishly, as soon as they were fairly started toward home. "I hoped Lucy wouldn't be such a fool as to tie herself down to such strait laced notions, even if the rest do, but they're all off the same piece, I've no patience."

"Nobody thinks you have," observed Harry, coolly.

"Now, Harry, I must say you ought to be ashamed of yourself, you have done little else all the evening but make yourself hateful."

"And what have you done, pray?"

"I haven't disputed everything you have said," Laura spoke like one who felt deeply aggrieved, but Harry only gave a low whistle, then adding, "You can supply the rest yourself, Laura. I won't waste my breath."

"Don't, I pray you, and it's a pity you hadn't grown more prudent of that valuable commodity sometime ago."

Laura was really provoked, and thus they rode on for some time, both preserving an uncomfortable silence, till, as if moved by a sudden impulse Harry said,

"I say, though, it's a pity that so pretty a girl as Lucy Day should be worked over into a whining, fussing, long faced old maid, just when she's fitted to be a real star in society. I used to hope to win her to share my fortunes, but the game's up that way now, I presume she looks upon me as a vile reprobate, hardly worth the prayers that are offered for such rascals as I am."

"I wish I could get her away from home for a while, I'd see what I could do to upset some of her notions. The most agreeable thing you've said today, is your wish to win Lucy as yours. I don't know of anybody I should prefer for a sister."

"Not even Sallie Clinton, with her style and diamonds?"

Harry could not refrain from quizzing, and Laura's answer was pettish in the extreme.

"I don't like Sallie Clinton, and you know it, and why you everlastingly contrive to bring her into the conversation is more than I can under stand. She's just a hateful thing, and the man who gets her will find her gold, with such a burden as she is, a miserable bargain."

"All envy, envy, sweet sister." Harry spoke in pretended reproof. "Miss Clinton is a jewel, her gold is only a fitting setting for such a gem, but seriously, Lucy Day, with poverty as her dowry, if she would only give

Temptation and Triumph 65

up her new notions, is more to my taste. She needs no gilding to make her shine."

Laura spoke, "Fred and John are coming out first class revivalists, only think, Harry, they have established prayer meetings about in the different school houses, and when no minister is present either one or the other of the Days takes the lead of the meeting. Fred's high notions of being a successful lawyer and statesman have all subsided, he'll be studying for the ministry yet."

"He's going to teach a common school this coming winter, and he actually told of it as though he felt proud of the fact," returned Harry. "I wonder what has become of his pride. When we entered college, he was decidedly the finest fellow and the best scholar in our class. He was so proud that 'twas sometimes said, when one lacked a comparison, 'as proud as Fred Day,' and now look at him, pretending to be content over his digging potatoes and husking corn, and happy in the thought of spending the winter teaching stupid urchins, bah! It makes me ashamed of his lack of spirit. I'd have speculated, or gambled, or done something for the money, but I should have gone in some way, good or bad, and he just gives all up and settles down."

"There is one thing I'm determined upon," declared Laura, as they drove up the tree, shaded avenue of their home.

"And what is that?" asked her brother.

"Why, to ask her over to spend a part, at least, of next week with me, and we'll have so gay a time that she'll wish for nothing better, as they pretend their religion is."

"Bravo for you! You're the prime article," exclaimed Harry, and lifted his sister to the ground.

Oh, Laura, Laura Howard! With your beautiful face and winning manners, how dark is the way in which your feet are straying. How wretchedly deaf are you to those words of Holy Writ that record the Master's assertion, that for him "who shall offend one of these little ones who believe in me, it were better for him that a millstone were hanged about his neck, and that he were drowned in the depth of the sea. Woe unto the world because of offenses! For it must needs be that offenses come, but woe to that man by whom the offense cometh!" Would it not be the most grievous way in which she could offend Lucy's trusting affection, if she should thus turn that affection into a snare leading to some sin of omission or of commission?

"What a happy day yesterday was! It does seem as though each Sabbath increased in blessedness!" Lucy Day and her sisters were variously employed in the great kitchen of the farm house, and Lucy in giving utterance to the above remark, could not repress a sign that she must so soon be far away again from the, beloved home circle.

"Yes, 'twas a happy day, indeed," answered Lottie.

Mary added, "The only thing that saddened me, was that we should most likely have you here only one Sunday more, it will seem harder than ever to have you gone."

"I dislike to have you go, too," said Anna. "But Grandma says, when I get to worrying about how we shall miss you, that, though she loves you better than ever, if that is possible, she shall feel safer about you, for you have got on the armor. If you only keep it bright by prayer and careful watchfulness, you won't need to fear but you'll be kept safely."

"Grandma is a dear old comforter, and you are a dear young one," Lucy answered, kissing her sweet young sister, as the girl stood fondly beside her, while the eyes of both glistened with tears. "I shall indeed," she said softly. "I have a strong Arm on which to lean, and I haven't any of those doubts and fears that hung darkly around me all last year. Now I only fear lest I shall do something to dishonor the cause of Christ, and fail of doing my duty, my whole duty. If I only knew that I should be kept from yielding to temptation, I should be almost perfectly happy."

"Perhaps, dear child," said her grandmother, who just then came in, "perhaps that very fear may be your safeguard from evil, for 'twill make you cling closer to the cross. Then you must be on the lookout for opportunities to do something for the Saviour, and those who labor for Him will be less likely to find employment in Satan's service."

"What a different motive I shall have in trying to do good! Last year I was so anxious to do something to merit God's favor, and thus find the peace I was seeking. Now I shall only be thankful that there is anything I can do for him, and shall feel that it's all just nothing when compared with what he has so freely done for me. What I once did from motives of duty, I shall now do from love. I hope I shall find plenty to do."

Lucy's voice quivered with earnestness, and the grandmother's tones were more than usually tremulous, as she said, "There is no lack of work in the Lord's vineyard, willing hands never need be idle, and His work brings this gladness with it. The more we do, the more we want to do, and the more we see to do, and all the while our hearts are expanding, and getting new stores of hope, and that perfect love which the Bible tells us, 'casteth out fear.'"

"Lucy, Lucy Day!" a merry voice summoned Lucy to the door. Down by the shaded gateway, Laura Howard had reined in her horse, and now sat, leaning forward in a light buggy, awaiting her friend's coming.

"The greetings of the day over," she explained. "I've come after you to spend the week with me. Annette Parsons and her sister and cousin, are to be at my home a part of the time, while Harry is expecting a trio of college friends to visit him, and I want you to come and have a good time with us."

"I don't know," Lucy hesitated.

"But I do," persisted Laura. "I have not the slightest idea of taking 'no', for my answer, so just run and get ready. That's a dear, and send Mary or Lottie to talk with me while you're making your preparations."

After a little delay, Lucy took her seat beside her friend, with the intention of returning home by the afternoon of Thursday, if not sooner.

"She won't be at home for a week," Laura asserted, as they drove away. "'Twas a shame to keep you cooped up at home all the time," she added. "I meant to take the matter into my own hands, if you and all your family are willing that you should make a perfect nun of yourself, I am not, and you won't have much of a chance to, while you're with me."

"I haven't been cooped up at all," exclaimed Lucy earnestly, "I have had the happiest time that any one need ask for. I only wish you could have been here on Grandma's birthday. Grandpa said it was a 'perfect blessing of a day,' and we all agreed with him."

"I dare say it was nice," answered Laura, "but how you can manage to exist with such a humdrum life, I can't imagine. I'm sure I couldn't, I should die before a month had passed."

"I find my life full of blessings, and as for dying from dullness, there's no danger of that, I assure you." Lucy felt almost hurt at her friend's tone, but she spoke very gently in reply.

"Are you engaged, positively, to return to Martinsville?" Laura asked presently.

"God willing, I hope to go back. I could not find a more pleasant situation and I am glad the people are so well satisfied I wish to return," answered Lucy.

"Are you really satisfied with such a life? I thought a year ago that you were too romantic, by half, but supposed you had got over it before this time. Are you still waiting for your character to perfect in this wonderful discipline of toil and sorrow? You remember you were very brave about what you was going to accomplish."

Lucy laughed pleasantly, and answered, "Oh, yes, I remember it all, and how you declared you would sit down and fold your hands, and starve, before you would go to work. Now I haven't really found the work so very hard. Do I look as though it had worn upon me?"

Laura looked at her fair face a moment before she answered. "Truth compels me to confess that you are prettier than ever, and with so much freshness and life about you, that you would be admired in the very highest society."

"Thanks, but spare my blushes." Lucy covered her face playfully, while Laura continued.

"Father told me last night that I might invite you to spend a year with me. He would treat you in all respects as a daughter, so you can just warn the Martinsville people that they can look out for another teacher, as I mean you shall never go back there."

"Oh, Laura!" Lucy looked the astonishment, which she failed of finding words to express, and her friend proceeded.

" 'Twill be so nice to have you with me all the time. Of course I have to stay at home some, and then I get so blue, with Harry gone, and so you'll be doing good, if that will help the matter any."

Lucy was puzzled. Duty and inclination seemed at variance, and Laura's last suggestion, that she should "be doing good," almost turned the scale. "I don't know what to say, nor how to thank you," she at last said, "must I decide today?"

"Certainly not, take your own time." Laura expected a favorable response to her offer, from Lucy's hesitation, and so the matter was dropped for the time.

Harry's friends had arrived during Laura's absence. In the afternoon, the other expected guests made their appearance, a conversation, made up of more gay nothings and flippant irreverence than Lucy had listened to for many long months, was commenced. Before the "goodnights" were uttered, for the first time the truth had dawned upon the young Christian's mind, that she was trifling with great trusts and putting her own peace of heart in peril if she consented to find her home among such follies for any length of time.

She caught the half-scornful smile with which Laura regarded her. When, on seeking the quiet of the chamber, which they were to share together, she sat down for a few moments' reading of the sacred volume before retiring for the night. When she knelt to offer her silent petition, she felt that the eyes, which watched her, were lit by no kindly sympathy.

Before the second day ended, Lucy was thoroughly tired, there was no vitality in a life like this. Unconsciously to herself, she had risen intellectually far above the plains whereon her friend was content to grovel, even while gaily imagining herself treading the very heights of earthly felicity. The struggle to find the truth had deepened Lucy's natural earnestness. While her constantly faithful preparation to meet the needs of her pupils, and lead them to see more beauty and meaning in school life and its exercises, had given her a love for nobler aims, than those which occupied the attention of the gay group with whom she was now connected.

On Wednesday, a new influx of visitors came from the city, and amid the constant and kind attentions shown her, the steady poise of the young girl's principles might have been lost, but for the light that, shining from above, made so plain all the perils that surrounded her. She was with them, and yet not of them, while the purity of her sweet face and the unstudied grace of look and motion came near making Laura envious, only that she plainly saw that the admiration excited was unsought by Lucy herself. Again and again had Laura, aided by her brother, urged upon Lucy the acceptance of Mr. Howard's generous offer, but her reply had been, "I must talk with my parents first."

Harry had breathed fiercely more than one oath, as the thought of their probable advice, for the gentle girl, in her Christian purity, had a charm for him, that was possessed by none else of his acquaintance. Plans for a gay winter in the city were canvassed, and what they deemed the strongest temptations were Lucy's surest warnings.

Laura Howard curled her beautiful lips in scorn at Lucy's "puritanism," as she was pleased to call it, and Harry did worse, but his swearing only helped to heap still higher his mountain of sins, and did Lucy no harm.

"I shall drift with the current, I am afraid," she said when at home once more. She told her loved ones of the offer she had received, while Grandpa answered, "Cling to the ark, my child, I doubt if this plan is for your best good, and then perhaps you will lose blessed chances of doing good. You must think of all this, and pray God to guide you in the path of highest usefulness."

"I have, Grandpa," she said, "and it seems as if my way lay through the open door of the Martinsville school room."

"Then go there, by all means," the old man exclaimed fervently, with his hand on his granddaughter's head, "we are always safest in the path of duty."

"Lucy, if you do not wish to leave home again, there is no need that you should. God has so kindly prospered us that there is no necessity for the rigid self-denial and struggle with which we commenced the year. There is plenty of home work for you, and my daughter knows how painfully we feel her absence, and how happy her presence makes us."

It was Mr. Day who spoke now, and Lucy, with a quick, impulsive movement, laid her cheek fondly against his, while she answered gently, "Dear Father, I would rather stay at home, but I can't help feeling that duty says, 'Go,' and if so, I ought to obey."

"Go then, and God bless you, and He will bless you," said her father solemnly, and so the decision was made.

Chapter IX
A Merry Christmas

To Mary Bradley the Christmas gathering was something so very delightful that many a gay belle might have envied the child. Her father had a lady friend make a new pink dress for Mary, which her father had provided for the occasion. She knew nothing about it till she was sent one evening to Mrs. Lane's, on some trivial errand, and found that lady prepared to "try on her dress," which had been cut by another which Mr. Bradley had carried over for the purpose. The dress, with its snowy ruffles at the throat and wrists, was wonderfully becoming, and tears almost blinded her father's eyes when he remembered how, one winter in the past, her dead mother had worn a similar dress, and looked, oh! So much as Mary looked now.

Won through the child's loving ministry to the seeking of salvation, the father felt that all he could do to make Mary happy, to cover the dark desolation of her worse than orphaned babyhood and early childhood, with the flowers of present happiness, was but a reasonable duty as well as a sacred pleasure. So he had quite recently been in the habit of giving her small sums of money that any simple want that he should overlook, or not understand, might be supplied.

Young Mary was very different from the Mary Bradley of the early spring, or even the Mary Bradley of berry-time. She had mourned over her lack of means to accomplish her wishes for others, however on the Tuesday evening before Christmas, sat in Dr. Osborne's sitting-room, with Alice busily engaged in putting in readiness various gifts, which Frank had volunteered to label for them.

A Merry Christmas

"Those are for Blanche Holton," Mary said, handing him a pretty pair of white mittens, with a delicate tuft of blue around the wrist. "I crocheted them for her, but I meant you to make your writing look different from your usual hand, and only say 'From a friend,' after her name, for perhaps she wouldn't be pleased to have me give her anything."

"She's a hateful old," but his mother's gentle, "Frank, Frank," nipped his bitter speech in the bud, and he turned to his writing.

"Let's take the scarves next, Mary," and Alice held up two long, warm tippets that for weeks they had been busy over, when chance offered the opportunity. "I'm afraid Father will be coming in and see them. Can you tell which is which?"

Mary pointed out a slight mistake in one. "That's the way I know mine. I made a blunder one night, and did not see it till I had knit quite apiece, and thought it wasn't worth while to pull it out for such a trifle. These mittens ought to be put out of sight, too."

The long winter evening wore on, and by and by came a pull at the bell. Mr. Bradley was announced, and on going out, Mary found she was to ride home in state, on a hand-sled. Frank gaily offered her the dinner bell to ring on her way home, so that she could have a sleigh ride in good earnest.

Thursday evening came cloudless, with a whole sky full of stars. When Mary and her father reached Dr. Osborne's, Alice having begged that she and Mary might go in company, they found that young lady already robed and waiting, watching their coming with eager face pressed against the window pane.

"Roses and violets," said Dr. Osborne, as the two girls stood side by side, Alice's blue dress as suitable in its adaptation to her delicate complexion, as was Mary's newly made dress to the richer shading of her happy face. "Let us hope that the rose may prove thornless, and the violet fragrant with the sweet perfume of a pure life."

"Roses are sweet, too, Father," said Alice, "and," added the affectionate child, "Mary is sweeter than any rose. Grandma Brewer said so the other day. I was telling her how we had been choosing flowers that we would love to be like, and Mary chose the rose, only she said she was afraid her life would never be as beautiful and sweet as the roses are, and then Grandma said that. There, I'm all ready."

It rivaled a scene in fairyland, that into which the party entered, while the music that filled the room seemed to come floating from afar, so low and tenderly it fell on the ear. Away up in the eastern end of the community hall hung a single lamp, like a star gleaming out of the surrounding gloom. While lower down, where the full blaze of light flashed upon the green tracery, shone forth the words, "Glory to God in the highest, and on earth peace, good will toward men." A cross here, an anchor there, with wreaths and drapings, appropriate mottoes, and passages from the scriptures, all formed from evergreen and laurel, decked the white walls.

Mary and Alice, with their small hands clasped fondly, almost held their breath in admiring wonder, while into their hearts like heavenly music fell the strains of, "While shepherds watched their flocked by night."

When the whole of the sweet old hymn had been sung, Alice whispered, "Doesn't it almost seem, Mary, as though we should see the angel coming?" Then Pastor Adams told them of the pleasant German customs of keeping Christmas. Martin Luther, when a poor little boy, chanted Christmas carols about the streets, with a band of young companions. Then little Katie Adams stood by her father's side, on the seat, so that all could see her, and repeated a beautiful translation of a German poem about the "Christ Child." So with singing and music, the recitation of poems that were the offspring of hearts attuned to Christmas rejoicing, and pleasant remarks from one and another present, the time sped, and then at last came the dispensing of the gifts. Pastor Adams prefaced with the expressed hope that all present should receive into their hearts, as a personal and permanent good, the knowledge of salvation through God's best, ever new, and ever precious Christmas gift to mankind, the holy and spotless Lamb of God. Whose advent did angels herald, and who, after his mission on earth being ended, went up into heaven to prepare a place of endless rest for those who here truly believe on and obey Him.

Bright eyes grew still brighter with expectation as Pastor Adams began handing out gifts. Mary watched eagerly till she saw the two scarves taken down and then the warm blood flooded her cheeks and Alice showed more than her usual number of dimples, when "Dr. Osborne," and "Mr. Stephen Bradley," sounded through the room. By and by the mittens shared the same fate, and the two little girls exchanged exultant glances. Then their names were called till they each had quite a pile of pretty gifts. Mary was almost ready to scream with delight when to herself, as well as Alice was given a beautiful muff and collar, of soft gray fur, Dr. Osborne's presents to the little girls. When two beautiful Bibles, bound in black and gold, were added to their treasures, she felt that her gladness was unbounded. She watched Grandma Brewer when the pretty tatting collar she had made for her kind old friend was handed her, and caught the pleasant smile in which she looked her thanks. She saw too, that Blanche Holton showed pleasure at the gift she had prepared for her, and the young girl's loving heart grew still happier in the thought that she had aided in the pleasure of the evening by her simple efforts for others. When the gifts had all been distributed, thanks were returned to God for the gladness of the evening, and then with the united singing of "Praise God from whom all blessings flow." The happy company dispersed.

"Oh, Father, did you give Alice and me the Bible?" asked Mary, when they were once more at home, and, too full of excitement for immediate sleep, she sat warming her feet and admiring her treasures. "How good you are, and Dr. Osborne, too! Alice says 'tis like having two fathers, you are both so kind to us. Grandma Brewer must have given me this nice warm hood, see how pretty the tassels are, and the writing in this book looks like Mr. Adam's. Wasn't it a happy time, Father?"

"Yes, my darling, it made me happy to see you enjoying yourself so well," answered her father.

"What have you got in that bundle?" Mary happened to spy her father's Christmas gifts on the table. Her curiosity was aroused at the sight of one package of which she knew nothing.

"I haven't opened it yet," Mr. Bradley said, "but supposed 'twas something more of my little girl's work."

"No, I don't know anything about that." Mary was watching eagerly the unfolding of the paper. "I gave you the scarf and the mittens, just as Alice did her father, and Mrs. Osborne got us each a nice handkerchief, and I gave mine to the doctor, and Alice gave hers to you."

"What is this? Oh, Mary! My murdered Mary!" Mr. Bradley was very pale, and the hot tears flashed down on a small picture he held in his hand. "It is your mother, Mary," he went on as Mary sprang to his side, "just as she looked that bright autumn day when we were married. How many times I have wished I had her picture for your sake as well as my own, but the only picture I ever had of her was accidentally lost just before she died." Then he opened the accompanying note, and Mary looked over his shoulder as he read,

"Only a few days before Mary Lisle became your wife, I was here and took a picture of her, in her fresh, bright beauty. I was here again at the time of her sad death. You will pardon my allusion to this, but I think this was one reason why, amid my accumulation of pictures, I have saved hers. A few weeks ago, while on a visit at my friend, Dr. Osborne, I met your little girl. Being struck by her resemblance to the picture in my possession, I made inquiries. Afterward, on mentioning the facts in regard to the picture, was told by the doctor, that Mary had told Alice how glad a picture of her mamma would make her and you, too. Having explained this much, will you accept the enclosed, with the best wishes of one who, like yourself, had been reclaimed from the dominion of intemperance. As well as my earnest prayers that the new life on which you have entered, may be as replete with the gladness of the Christian's peace, as it is possible for God to make it?"

More than once Mr. Bradley had paused to wipe away the tears that dimmed his sight. On Mary's sweet face tears and smiles mingled, and when they learned that all this loving kindness was shown by a stranger, Mary said, looking up earnestly, "God must have told him to send it to you. Oh, how kind God makes everybody!" The gift was a small but exquisitely finished photograph, set into an oval frame of black, it having been retaken and enlarged from the one in the artist's possession.'

A Merry Christmas

"How beautiful she was!" said the child softly, and the father thought how wonderfully alike the two faces were, the pictured one of the mother, and the fair young face bent over it.

It was late the next morning when Mary awoke, and hastily dressing, her heart and lips running over with thanksgiving, she ran down stairs to find breakfast all prepared, while her father sat quietly reading.

"I thought I would let you sleep, my child," he said, "it was very late last night when you went to bed, and I wanted you to feel bright today. I have invited a young lady to take a sleigh ride with me, and shall want you to go, too." Mary looked bewildered; she didn't exactly like the idea of having a third party to share her father's attentions. "Don't you want to go?" he asked, half smiling at her puzzled look.

"Yes, indeed, father, I should like the ride, but,"

"But what? Don't you want Alice to go, too?"

"Alice, is it Alice you mean?" and now her look and voice were alike joyful. "That will be splendid. Where are you going? I never once dreamed of having such a merry Christmas. Oh! I forgot all about it, you astonished me so. I wish you a 'Merry Christmas.'"

"I trust it will be a peaceful one, such as I have not known for years," he answered, and then they sat down to breakfast. Prayer and praise hallowed the humble home, each morning and evening now, and this morning there seemed more than usual to thank God for. Then, while Mary was getting ready, Mr. Bradley went for a conveyance, and the girl, left to herself, filled the old house with gushes of melody as she busied herself about her preparations. Then came the jingle of bells, and Alice, full of glee, came bounding into the room.

"You're going to our house to dine," she said, "your father has promised my mother, and I've got a whole pail full of nice things to carry that poor sick Mrs. Staples, and your father says he'll carry us around to see her."

"How nice!" said Mary, her face all aglow. "I mean to ask father if I can't carry her some of our great red apples."

"Yes, child, and here are some other things for you. When I heard Alice's plan, I thought you would want to have a share in the pleasure, and so bought a pound of figs and a dozen oranges," and Mr. Bradley bent to receive his daughter's grateful kiss.

"Grandma Brewer said," continued Alice, "that when I wished you a 'Merry Christmas,' I must wish you a dozen for her, and to tell you besides, that she wanted us to take tea with her New Year's night. Miss Day and mother are going, too."

"Oh, how bright and beautiful it is!" Mary exclaimed, as they drove off, far down by the now leafless woods. Where the cool, deep shadows crept so thickly in the summer time, out over the level road through the meadows, where the snow lay on either side in gently undulating waves, starred with millions on millions of diamonds, dazzling in their frail beauty. "I never knew what a 'merry Christmas' was before. It seems just like a dream to me. If it is, however, I hope shan't wake up just yet." Mary nestled down closely beside her father, every now and then leaning forward to catch a glimpse of Alice's happy face, on the other side.

"I always have a merry time at Christmas, but this seems a happier one than I ever knew before," said Alice. "What did you use to do when you was a little boy, Mr. Bradley?"

"Just about the same as children do now, only instead of having a Christmas tree, I hung up my stocking beside the open fire-place. When I was quite small, I believed what they told me, that St. Nicholas came down the chimney and brought my presents, and filled my stocking, himself."

"Did you really believe he drove around with a team of reindeer, and his sleigh piled up full of nice things?" asked Mary.

"Yes, I thought it all true, till one night I lay awake with the determination of seeing the jolly saint. After I thought the rest of the family was in bed, I crept softly down stairs in the bright moonlight. I remember how clear and cold the night was, and when I opened the kitchen door, there was my mother, busy at work, filling the row of little stockings that hung side by side at the fireplace. She turned around as I went in, and said,

'Why, Stephen, what are you up for?'"

"And you told her you wanted to see St. Nicholas?" asked Alice.

"Yes, and she laughed at me, and when I cried, she took me in her lap, and tried to comfort me. She said she was sorry that anybody had made me believe such a foolish story. Though a little sorry to have so pleasant a belief shaken, I was more than a little proud the next morning, to be able to tell the rest how much wiser I was than they. Here we are at the house of Mrs. Staples, you mustn't make a long call, for we have quite a long drive before us."

Mr. Staples was, himself, at home, and came gruffly to the door at the sound of the bells. He softened a little at the, "I wish you a merry Christmas," of the little girls, and held the door open for them to enter.

"Yes, 'tis a fair sort of a morning," he returned, in answer to Mr. Bradley's salutation, "but very cold. I wonder if you can't find anything else to do but ride about. I wish I could find time for such nonsense as all this nonsense and fuss about Christmas. You're getting into grand company, eh? Once I was good enough for you to associate with. Now when I'm enough sight better fitted, by good rights, for being taken notice of, for I hadn't got any blood on my hands, people shun me like a python, and you are treated like as if you was a gentleman, instead of being just out of jail."

A deep red burned in Stephen Bradley's cheeks, and his lips had been firmly pressed together. Now, as the man paused, he said gently, "I never meant to treat you unkindly, James. You and I were old school mates, and many a day have we spent nutting or fishing together. I have sinned greatly, and since I came back here, I have not sought for fellowship. I tried to be independent and stand aloof from everybody, but God led kind hearts to pity and to pray for me. He gave me the constant and blessed lesson of a Christian child's daily life, and He so touched my hard, wicked heart, by the power of His Holy Spirit, that I could no longer resist its influence. Now I am His for life, and hope to be with Him through all eternity." James Staples, half-drunk as he was, looked stupidly at the speaker, and with a prolonged whistle went away towards the woods, with his ax on his shoulder.

"In the name of the great horned frog, I should like to know what has come over Bradley," he muttered as he went slowly on. "Once he would have fired up, and pitched right into a fellow, if they had sassed him as I did, now he's as meek as any old granny."

In the meantime, the little girls were cheering the sick woman by their account of last night's gladness. By the display of their presents, which they had worn, while they spread out on the table beside her bed, their various offerings for her, so that, when she was left alone, she might be cheered thereby. Oh, how glad they made her, and how they all day remembered her fervent, "God bless you, and he will bless you, of that I'm sure, you precious darlings!" as they bade her "good-bye."

Then the horse sprang on again, as though he was ready to aid all in his power toward the day's pleasure, and the children chatted, and Mr. Bradley now and then joined in their gay talk. Though calmly happy, his life had yet so many sad remembrances, that it sometimes seemed to him almost a crime to be happy. Only when he looked away from himself, his own wrong doings and weakness, and felt the clasp of the strong hand that he knew was ever ready to hold him up, did he feel that even for him and for such as he had been, pardon and peace were possible.

On they went, past farmhouses where the smoke curled up lazily through wide chimneys, and where, through the broad windows, they caught glimpses of happy family gatherings. Here seeing a cherry-cheeked child watching them pass, there discovering a darling baby, crowing and dancing at the rough and tumble merriment of children playing in the snow before the house, now meeting gay parties out sleigh-riding like themselves.

"Did you see how pale Blanche Holton looked last night?" Alice asked presently. "Father said, this morning that she was quite sick, and that she was dreadfully unhappy, don't you pity her?" Mary answered,

"Poor Blanche! I noticed she didn't study much at school yesterday. I'm sure I pity her, ever and ever so much. If she only had a home to go to now, 'twould be so much better."

A Merry Christmas

After a while, they stopped to warm them. A nice gay time they had, eating nuts and apples, in the cozy parlor of the little country café. Then as the sun had crept up high in the heavens, the horse's head was turned homeward, just when Mrs. Osborne's dinner was all ready, and Frank had grown tired watching for them, they drove up to the door. Then answering Frank's, "Helloo! Young women, just in time," with shouts of glee, and then they came in, rosy with the cold.

Just at sunset Dr. Osborne carried Mary home, her father having gone sometime before. Thus, "too happy to mind being tired," she had told her father upon entering her home. Mary ended the first real "Merry Christmas" she had ever enjoyed with a fervent prayer of thankful rejoicing, and went peacefully to sleep.

Chapter X
Forgiveness and It's Fruits

Poor Blanche Holton tossed wearily on her sick bed, moaning fretfully, and longing to see her absent mother, a wish, alas that could never be realized on earth, for Mrs. Holton was fast fading away, and could not come to see her sick child. Indeed, Blanche was to have gone to pay a brief visit at her grandfather's, and see her almost dying mother, when stricken down by illness, herself. Her older sisters, like Blanche herself, had never received the training needful to fit them for the cheerful acceptance of a life of self-dependence. They made their trials harder by bitter repinings and the neglect of the duties required of them, and were thus less considerately treated than would otherwise have been the case. About the time that Julia was summoned to watch over her mother's deathbed, Etta, having lost her situation, married a reckless adventurer, and followed him and his fortunes to a distant city. So there were none of Blanche's relatives who could come to care for her and in her weakness and suffering, she felt like one deserted by all she loved.

For several weeks she was severely ill, and though Mrs. Benton did everything in her power for her comfort, she missed the loving care that had so shielded her from infancy. "Will she get well?" How many times Dr. Osborne's ears were greeted by this question, and at last he was rejoiced to be able to answer, "I hope so, if nothing new occurs, I believe so."

He had not thought it best for Mary or Alice to visit her, while tossed and burned with fever, lest the sickness prove contagious, but many a bright flower or fragrant green leaf had been sent by them to the sick girl. Now they waited anxiously for the time when they might see her again. A knowledge of her sufferings would have rooted out of Mary's heart all remembrance of her former unkindness, even if any such feeling had been harbored therein, which was not the case. Glad indeed were the two girls when, one pleasant afternoon in February, they started for an hour's call on the lonely girl. Once or twice her sister had been with her for a few hours, but as their mother yet lingered, it was impossible for her to stay long, and so the poor child brooded over her loneliness till the doctor thought it retarded her recovery. When Mary and Alice entered her room, the quick start of delight, that called up a brief smile to her pale lips, proved even more than words her pleasure at seeing them.

"How good you are, girls!" she said, as they sat down beside her. "I was so lonely this afternoon that I didn't know what to do, 'tis such a long time to lie here sick."

"Yes," said Mary, smoothing back Blanche's hair with her soft, warm palm. "I don't wonder you get lonely, but we've come to cheer you up, and we're coming real often now. Father told me I might invite you to come and make me a good long visit, so you must get well quick, for I'm in a hurry to have you come."

"And my father says," added Alice, "that the happier you are, the quicker you will get well. See what we have brought you!" and from her muff Alice produced a bunch of bright-hued verbena blossoms, arranged around a sprig of geranium leaves, while Mary's gift was a great rosy-cheeked apple. Blanche turned her head away, and covered her face with her poor pale hands, while she shook with sobs.

"Why, dear Blanche, what is the matter?" Mary asked, softly, "do you feel badly at anything we have said?"

"Oh, I've treated you so, and felt so ugly toward you, Mary, and I've made fun of Alice, too, and now you act just as though you loved me, both of you," and her lips quivered piteously.

"So we do," they both exclaimed, while Mary added, "I never thought of remembering anything you ever said, or did, to trouble me. I only hoped you would love me sometime, as well as I did you."

"And you forgive me?" Blanche asked, her eyes still filled with tears.

"I will forgive you, as if there wasn't anything to forgive," was the answer, as Mary pressed a kiss on Blanche's forehead.

"Now we'll have a happy time, talking, I've got lots to tell you, Blanche." Alice took up the broken thread of talk, and weaving it in and out with all the pleasant things they could remember, an hour slipped away before they were aware. Then Mrs. Benton came softly in, and found Blanche looking so bright and happy, that she declared they were doing more good than the doctor, and so left them alone again. For that reason, their one hour call grew into two, and then when they were preparing to go, Blanche said, her eyes filling anew with tears, "I wish I was as good as you are, Mary, I have felt sorry so many times since I have been lying here sick. When I thought how badly I had treated you, and sometimes when I knew they were afraid I should never get well, it seemed as if I could not die without asking you to forgive me. You gave me those nice mittens, didn't you? I have never worn them, but when I got to feeling so badly, I would think of the mittens, and try to get some comfort in the thought that you couldn't quite hate me, or you wouldn't have given them to me."

"Hate you! Why, dear Blanche, I never once thought of such a thing," exclaimed Mary. Blanche in her weak tones went on.

"I hope I never shall treat anybody so again."

"Don't you ask God to help you?" asked Mary.

"I've tried to say the Lord's prayer," Blanche answered, "but we never had prayers at our house, and Mr. Benton never prays, and somehow I felt away off so far from God, I couldn't feel that he heard me when I tried to pray."

"Oh, but he will." Alice was all earnestness.

While Mary added in her more quiet tones, "God always hears us when we go to him, you must keep praying, dear Blanche, he'll be sure to answer you, I know he will, he does me."

"Oh, but you're good," said Blanche, sadly. "I'm very bad, and that makes a great difference."

Forgiveness and It's Fruits

"We aren't any of us good, only as God helps us to be," Mary replied. "We can't make ourselves good. God forgives our sins because Christ died for us. If we are sorry and repent of them, and go to him and ask him to pardon us, and then He never leaves us to go on alone, just as long as we ask Him to help us, never in the world."

"Alice, we must go. Good-bye, you dear, sick Blanche, get well quick, so I can have that visit. I want to show off my housekeeping." Mary bent over Blanche and lovingly kissed her.

"Oh, how much I do thank you for coming!" said the girl, as she kissed them both. "I thank you both for all your kindness, and you'll come again, won't you?"

"Indeed we will," they both exclaimed. Then they were going out, but Mary ran back and whispered tenderly, "Don't forget that God will help you, dear Blanche, if you only ask Him, and I shall pray that you may be taught to love Him. Then all the hard things in your life will seem easier to bear."

Out into the clear winter sunshine the two girls hastened, little knowing how much sunshine they had left behind them.

"How bright you look, Blanche!" said Mrs. Benton, going a little later into the girl's room. "We ought to have let your friends come sooner, if they are going to do you so much good."

"Do you believe angels ever live here on earth, Mrs. Benton?" asked Blanche, as the lady sat down beside her.

"Why, what a question! What made you think of such an idea?"

"Mary Bradley made me think of it, and I really believe, if angels ever live here, she is one. Oh, Mrs. Benton, you don't know how I used to treat her, call her a beggar, and all that, and try to make the other girls dislike her, and I never heard her say anything unkind back again, or knew of her doing any mean act. She's all the time treated me just as though she loved me, and wanted me to love her. I used to wonder at her, and wish sometimes that she would get mad, and talk back again, so that I should have some excuse, but she never did, and I hated to have other people like her so well. I've been just as ugly, and you can't guess how ugly. I asked her to forgive me and this is the way she put it, 'I will forgive you, as if there isn't anything to forgive.' She loves me and wants me to come and make her a long visit, as soon as I get able. Isn't it very strange?'"

"Mary is a Christian, that is the secret," said Mrs. Benton, "and I only wish all who profess religion were as faithful and earnest as she is. There's been a wonderful change in her father, and when he related his experience before the church, he said that Mary's influence, under God, had been the means of his salvation. My husband, little as he cares about such things, says, if anything would make him believe in Christianity, it would be little Mary Bradley's life."

"Mary is truly walking in the light." Dr. Osborne came in, in time to catch Mrs. Benton's last words, and he added, "Eternity will alone reveal the blessed results of the influence of a life like hers. It is a lesson to older followers of the Lamb, to see her humble and consistent example."

"I wish I could be half as good," Blanche said softly. The kind doctor sat down beside her, holding her thin hand in his strong but gentle grasp, while he told her it was not only possible for her to be one-half, but wholly as good as Mary was, by learning, as Mary had, the lesson of Christ's pardoning mercy, and the peace that follows a personal acceptance of it. "My dear child," he added, "the best thing I could wish for you, would be to see you following Mary's example of giving your heart to Jesus, and devoting yourself to His service."

Blanche laid her cheek fondly against the kind hand that still held hers, and said, very gently, little like her old way of speaking, "I do want to be like Mary, but I've been so naughty, and 'tis so hard to do good."

"God will help you," he replied, and then he added, playfully, "I suppose after having two nurses this afternoon, there was little need of your having a visit from me. I wonder what magic they've been using; I haven't seen you look so nicely for weeks. We shall have you out sleigh riding soon. If you only get able to go, I'll be happy to give you a ride, a nice long one, one of these fine mornings."

"I guess it was the magic of love," answered Blanche, "for they both told me they loved me, and I don't deserve it one bit. Somehow I felt glad, so glad I can't tell you, even while I was feeling sorry to think I was so bad."

"The magic of love, eh? Wonder if I should grow better looking as fast as you have, if somebody should tell me that they loved me," the doctor said, quizzingly. "I guess I'll ask someone to try the effect of such a declaration upon me."

Blanche laughed musically, a happier sound than had issued from her lips from months, and after a few more cheering words the doctor took his departure.

"How kind people are to me!" Blanche said to herself. "I never thought anything about it before, perhaps I don't remember, but it seems to me they've grown kinder to me than they used to be, though Mary never was uncharitable or unkind."

Poor child! She did not know that the difference was in her own feelings, that just now a little stray beam of God's pure light was shining into her darkened heart, and things unnoticed before, now lay plain and beautiful before her.

Then she went quietly to sleep as she had not slept before for many nights, feeling so much gladness in the thought that Mary had forgiven her, and that love was a bond between them which she meant to do all in her power to strengthen.

Mary and her father had taken the vows of God upon them early in the New Year. Stephen Bradley, earnest in whatever he undertook now that this earnestness was consecrated to God's service, seemed a new man indeed. He would hardly have been recognized by those who had know him as the reckless youth of other years, or the sad, heart-crushed man who had come back from his dreary imprisonment, determined to resist temptation and to stand strong, alone and unaided, seeking and expecting neither friends nor friendship. Constant at church and prayer meeting, active in the Sabbath school, a faithful worker in each and every department of labor, he was what he had never expected to be, comparatively happy. He now thought of his sins as forgiven, and if forgiven, he felt it wrong to devote time that should be used for noble efforts, in a useless repining over the past and the deeds of the past. There was that which he never could forget, and never cease to regret, but his hope was strong in God, and he left it all with Him.

Lucy Day, too, had owned her Saviour before the world, and rejoiced in being numbered among his followers. "Dearer than ever," her pupils said she was, and, oh! how much happier than during the year previous! Then, many duties were penances; now, they were privileges and joys. Her home remembrances were sweet, and her home tidings no less so, while her daily life was at once prayer and praise. Prayer, for she constantly uplifted her heart to God in petitions for strength and guidance, praise, for it was in thankfulness that her blessings were welcomed, as from God's gracious hand.

Now and then, her sisters, in their letters, mentioned Laura Howard and the gay life she was living, and how studiously she had avoided them since Lucy's return to Martinsville. Once, a letter brought the tidings of Harry's disgraceful expulsion from the college of which he was a student, in consequence of a vile attempt, in which he and several others had united, to injure some poor but worthy students, vastly the superiors of the reckless young aristocrats who were leagued against them.

It could not but sadden Lucy to hear so unpleasant a report of those once so dear to her, but in this instance she carried her regret and sorrow, where she had found the only sure source of comfort, to the foot of the Cross. She had received an advantageous offer of a situation as teacher in a school of higher grade than the one in which she was now engaged, but so sincere and abundant were the desires to have her remain, and the expressions of grief at the very thought of her leaving, and felt her heart newly linked to her Martinsville friends, by these expressions of their confidence and esteem.

Late in February, Blanche came to pay that long-talked-of visit to Mary. It was evident to Dr. Osborne, that only the most careful attention, and freedom from anxiety, would ever win back the flush of health to the young girl's cheeks. And as the Benton family had kindly cared for her through all the weeks of her illness, bearing the by no means inconsiderable expense incurred, she felt that it was too much for her to expect to remain there longer. Her mother had died quite recently, and her older sister, herself frail in health, had gone wearily to her work once more, while the two younger children remained with the grandparents, whose scanty means were taxed to their utmost by past and present demands.

Mary's heart was full of sympathy, and her father, no less interested, extended a cordial invitation to Blanche to remain with them as long as she could feel contented. The poor girl was sincerely thankful, and humbly accepted the kind offer. She was learning in the school of affliction, and to those around her was growing more and more lovable every day. Even Frank Osborne, strong in his once averred dislikes as he was, confessed that the word "hateful" no longer applied to her. Still farther added, as a proof that he now believed her improvement possible, that if she went to stay with Mary Bradley, she was sure to come out all right in the end, saying, "Mary has such a way with her, that people grow good in her company in spite of themselves."

As for Blanche, untaught as she had been in the truths of religion, she, in the long hours that she had often to spend alone, mused on her talks with Mary and Dr. Osborne. Often she led the conversation to that once despised theme, the way of pardon and peace through Christ. She was a sincere seeker and sometimes her friends felt that in her heart they could plainly perceive the uprising of the blade, which in due time should become "the ear, and then the full corn in the ear." But as yet she dared not call herself a Christian, though her Bible was very dear to her, and prayer her daily watchword.

The days of the beautiful springtime came, and Blanche was still an inmate of Stephen Bradley's home. She was very weak yet, and often felt discouraged as to her ever fully regaining her health, but Dr. Osborne comforted her with the hope of her being better when the summer should come again.

"Dear, dear Mary, how shall I ever thank you for all your kindness?" were words often on her lips.

Mary would then promptly answer her with, "Don't try, I get the thanks as I go along. It's just like having a sister to have you here."

But as the days wore on, a look of constant sadness settled down over Blanche's face and all Mary's cheering words and loving smiles failed to dissipate it. Mary left her alone one morning for a little while, and when she returned, she found Blanche having what children call "a good cry."

"Why, what is the matter?" she exclaimed, "have you heard any bad news?" and she went down on her knees beside the weeping girl, putting her arms fondly around her.

"I didn't mean you should see me, but oh! Mary, I am so sad, I am such a helpless burden, and I don't seem to get one bit better. I've been thinking," and the girl sobbed convulsively, "that I ought to go to the almshouse. There's no one to take care of me, Julia is hardly able to earn her board, and she certainly can't do anything for me, and there doesn't seem to be anybody I can go to."

"You needn't go anywhere." Mary was holding her cheek against the tear-stained one of Blanche. "You can just stay where you are, we don't feel that you are a burden by any means. Father was saying, only last night, that he dreaded to have you leave us, we should miss you so much."

"But I can't do you any good, and just think how many steps you have had to take for me."

"And think how you have helped me sew. I've been talking with Father, and we've concluded that when school commences again, I won't go only afternoons. It's pretty hard work to keep house and go to school, too. Then I shall have my strawberry-bed to take care of, and I mean to have a famous flower garden. If you'll only stay contented, I shan't have to leave you alone only a little while in the afternoon. We can study the lessons together, and when you get stronger, we'll work out of doors together, and, and, why, Blanche, I don't see how I can get along without you!"

"What's all this, Blanche? Are you threatening to run away, and Mary on her knees pleading to have you stay?" and Dr. Osborne stepped in through the open door where, unperceived, he had caught the greater share of the conversation. "I'm just in time to settle all difficulties," he went on. "Mary, I'll cross question you first. What have you been doing to Blanche, to make her cry so?"

Mary laughed heartily at his conical look of mock dignity, and said, "I haven't been doing anything, sir, but Blanche imagines she is a trouble, and was talking about going to the almshouse, and I was telling her how I want to have her stay, that's all."

"That's your story! Now, Blanche, give us your version of the affair. It is necessary to hear both sides of the story."

"Why, it's about as Mary said, Doctor. I have been here so long that I really feared I was a burden, and I didn't know what to do, so I was crying. Mary got home sooner than I thought she would and found me. Then she was talking, just as she always does, so well, that it made me feel ashamed of myself, after all I have done in the past to trouble her. I've been real mean, and if I could only do something that would show her how sorry I am, I should be so glad."

"Just forget it, then, as I have, I love you dearly, Blanche, and as for your being sorry, I want you to forget that there is such a word, and be happy here."

"I don't know anywhere else I could be happy, but I want to do something to show my thankfulness. I want to get well," Blanche added what once she would not have thought of, "if God is willing, so that I can do something for Mary, and everybody else who is so good to me."

"My dear child," the doctor had a grave, sweet way, that almost compelled one to trust him and find comfort and strength in his words, "the happier you try to be, the sooner you will be able to help others. Though I doubt much if our dear little Mary here, ever thinks she takes one step too many in helping and caring for you, eh, Mary?"

There was an answer in Mary's smile as well as in her words. "I never think anything about it at all, we never do for those we love, do we? I'm as glad as can be to do anything for anybody, and still gladder for Blanche, because I know how to pity her, and feel for her better than most folks would."

There were tears in the soft eyes that looked up at the doctor's reply, "God gives us all a mission, dear children, and he gives different ones to different people. Some have to work hard, and some have to just lie still and suffer, and while, if done for God's glory, the work is true service, just as much so is the suffering that is patiently endured. Someone writes, 'They also serve who only stand and wait.' That is what you can do now, Blanche, and if you are faithful in this, God may give you something else to do, by and by, in his own good time."

Blanche said, a sweet look stealing over her pale, young face, "I sometimes think God has pardoned my sins, only I can't tell just when I first began to think so, as I have heard some people tell that they can. I have been praying ever so hard for Him to forgive my wickedness. I shouldn't feel afraid to die now, and once I should, and I do love to pray and read the Bible. The hymns that Mary sings so much seem just as though they were made on purpose to comfort me."

"God does not work in all hearts alike," answered the doctor, much moved at the simple words of the girl. "We are not all constituted alike, but the fruits of the Spirit are the same in all, and your feelings are such as one redeemed from the dominion of sin would possess. You say you are not afraid to die. Do you think you are any better now than when you were first taken sick, and that this makes you safer?"

"Oh no, sir, I don't trust in that. I should never think of letting myself be happy one moment if I had got to make myself good, and get to Heaven that way. I know we can't save ourselves. I read a great deal since I've been so weak, and Mary had read to me, and you know you have told me, and so has the minister, that we must trust in Christ alone, that He died for us, and that His blood alone could wash away our sins, and I never thought of any other way. I've only been afraid that I was so wicked that He wouldn't listen to me, if I did pray. Then I read about the thief on the cross, and how Christ promised to save him, and about Paul, too, and how he persecuted the people who believed on Jesus, and then how he was converted and how much good he did. I have thought sometimes that maybe He would save me, and let me get well to labor for Him, not as

St. Paul did, I don't mean that, but to do little things for Him."

"And you would have felt happy if it had not been for this trouble about its being your duty to go to the almshouse?"

"I think I would sir, and once in a while even that seemed as good as I deserve, and I tried to think that if God saw that it was best, I would be willing to go, through I didn't want to go. Do you suppose that was wrong?"

"No, I don't think it wrong, by any means. I certainly can't say that I should really want to go. It was perfectly natural that you should feel badly about going, and, my poor child," he added, very tenderly, "I don't believe you'll have to go."

"No, indeed, we shan't let her go, if we live and are prospered, it makes me very happy to have her here. I had to be alone so much that Father thinks it a great deal better for me to have somebody with me."

Blanche laid her head down against the high back of her rocking-chair, returning Mary's smile with one of such sweet content, that the doctor asked, "You will try and be happy and gain strength, won't you, now that all these fears about a home are set aside for the present?"

"I'll try, and I'm sure, with so much kindness shown me, I ought to be contented. Just now I feel as I have a few times before this, so tired, and just as though somebody was resting me, just as I used to feel when I was a little girl, and had been at play all day. I would come in so dreadfully tired, and mother would take me up in her lap, and hold my head close down against her. After a little while I would feel as well and happy as ever, and maybe jump down and run off to play again. And now it seems as if my heart was to be rested in the same way."

"I will strengthen thee, yea, I will uphold thee with the right hand of my righteousness.' The truth of this promise is coming home to you, Blanche. And now I must go, but first I want to kneel and thank God with you for the good hope with which He has blessed you."

When the doctor had gone, Mary came back to Blanche, and throwing her arms fondly about her neck, said with earnestness, "I am happier than ever now. I thought you were thinking about God, but I didn't know that you loved Him so well. We shall have better times than ever together, and Father will be so glad too."

Mary found an opportunity to tell her father of the forenoon's conversation. That night, when the girls were preparing to retire, he called Blanche to him, and, drawing her affectionately to his arms, kissed her as he had his own daughter. He told her that, as long as he had a home, she might claim it as hers, and that henceforth he should consider her as his daughter, to take care of as he took care of Mary. Blanche was too choked for words, but she returned his caress lovingly, and followed the happy Mary up stairs.

"Sister Blanche," whispered Mary, as they nestled down on their pillows.

"Yes, and what a lesson I needed, and what a lesson God has taught me!" returned Blanche. "Just look back and see how proud I was, and how I made fun of you, and wouldn't associate with you, because, forgive me for speaking about it, your father had been in jail. Now I have to remember this, and feel that I am dependent on you for a home, while my father is wandering, I don't know where, and if he could be found, would have to be put into prison, most likely for the rest of his life. How I do wish I could just know where he is, and if he is sorry for what he did, and wants God to forgive him!"

"We'll pray for him," said Mary. "God has led my father to love Him, and He can yours. I'll help you pray, and you know what we don't know and can't find out about, we must leave with God, for He always knows what is best for us all."

The next morning Mary was busy at work, singing like a lark, when a rap called her to the door, where she was surprised to find Mr. Staples.

"Will you do something for me?" he asked in a quieter manner than usual.

"Certainly, if I can," Mary answered, in some astonishment.

"Well, then, will you go and get the minister to come down to our house? *She* is worse, and *she* wants to see him, and I ain't acquainted with the minister, and perhaps he would come quicker if you should ask him. *She'd* be dreadful glad."

"Do you mean your wife? I hadn't heard that she was worse," Mary replied.

"O' course I mean her, *she's* all I've got to home, and the doctor says *she's* a'most used up, ain't going to last much longer."

She seemed to be an ample title by which to designate his wife, and even this was an improvement on the usual "old woman," and was used out of respect to Mary, whom the rough man held in more esteem than he would have been willing to confess. So Mary hurried after Pastor Adams, and a few hours later, the minister came in and gave them the understanding, that Mary felt could not be looked upon as sorrowful, that poor Mrs. Staples was released from her earthly suffering and had gone peacefully to sleep.

"She told me to bid you farewell," he continued, "and bade me say also, that, for the last six months, you had been her greatest earthly comfort, and that she felt God would bless you for it all."

The next day was appointed for the funeral, and Mr. Bradley and Mary went. When the moist turf, just tinged with the early green, was laid over the rough coffin, Mary thought how beautiful was the hope that, when the weary earthy frame had returned to its native clay, there was the comforting assurance that those who believe and seek salvation through Christ Jesus, are welcomed into the mansions that He has gone to prepare for them that love Him.

A week passed, and Mr. Staples again made his appearance, this time bringing a small trunk containing a few articles of clothing, some books, and other keepsakes of trifling value. Also saying, as he gave them to Mary, "She made me promise to bring these traps to you, and so I've brought them today, for I'm going to pull up stakes and tramp. I should have gone long ago if it hadn't been for her, and now she's gone, and I shan't stay here any longer."

"I hope you will be prospered, sir," Mary said, as, after she had thanked him for the gifts, he turned to depart.

"I guess you're the only one who'll wish Jim Staples any prosperity, but I've a fancy that your wish will do me about as much good as anybody's, for I believe you are downright good, and 'taint everybody who pretends to be, that I'd say that of. Good-bye, and if you've a mind to say a prayer for me sometimes, maybe God will hear it, and I shall get to be better after a while. Most likely I shan't ever see you ag'in, but I hope you'll have what you deserve, a happy life. If you wouldn't mind shaking hands with me, I would take it kindly, 'twill make me feel that I have one friend.'

Mary laid her little warm hand in his, and said, "Yes, indeed, Mr. Staples, I shall remember to pray for you, and I hope you will learn to love God. He will be better than any earthly friend to you, I shall pray that you may."

"And her prayers always seem to be answered, so I believe God will lead you to Him yet, and then you'll be happy if you are alone." The man turned quickly round to where Blanche's pale face looked out from her rocking chair at these words.

Mr. Staples said, as if thinking aloud, "I need something to make me happy, bad enough," then turned away and went slowly out of sight.

"I think he'll find Jesus, sometime, don't you, Blanche?" Mary asked, watching him, as he went.

"Yes, I think he will, it seems as though everybody you pray for finds Him."

Chapter XI
Shadows and Sunshine

"Mary!" At the unusual sound of her father's voice at that hour in the morning, Mary Bradley dropped the broom that she was wielding and hurried down stairs. Her father met her at the door. He seemed calmly determined upon something which he was desirous yet almost fearful to lay before her, and the girl said, with a quiver of apprehension running through the sweetness of her voice,

"What is it, Father?"

"Can you spare me, Mary, spare me for Truth's sake and the Right?"

Mary grasped the back of the chair near her. Except that the red faded from cheek and lip, she was calm as she replied, "You haven't enlisted, have you, Father?"

The man went on, while the color came and went in his daughter's expressive face, "There's a new call for three hundred thousand more, and I must go, I feel it is a sacred duty. I kept from going on your account, my darling, but now my very heart seems beating a summons to the ranks for the sake of freedom."

"Father," and the sweet face reflected the brave heart that yet so yearningly loved her only parent, "Father, not for one instant would I hinder you, if you think it your duty."

Then the tears welled up from the depths of the soul that consented to such a sacrifice, and shivering with suppressed feeling, she sprang forward into her father's outstretched arms.

Eight years had passed since Mary first yielded her heart to her Saviour and promised to live for His glory. What seemed a hope, faint but enduring, to her backward glance, now was so much a blessed certainty that she could sometimes say that it really seemed to her as though her heaven had indeed begun below, since God had so crowned her life. Not only with an abundance of earthly comforts, but with that still greater blessing, the constant joy of His presence.

At nineteen, Mary Bradley was beautiful and well educated, and the joy of the home she made so delightful to her father. Blanche Holton, two years Mary's senior, had only left their home to find another with the very one of all others they would have chosen for her, a young Christian merchant, and for the last year had lived a few miles distant, happy and beloved.

The old home had been enlarged, improved and beautified, till it would have been hard for anyone to recognize, who had not seen it since the days when, tenantless, or worse than tenantless, filled with some herd of miserable vagabonds, who prowled around nightly, it had been deemed a blot on the fair landscape.

"Home, sweet, sweet home." Mary sang it very often, and felt it a rightful title for their home nest, and now her sunshine suddenly and strangely shaded into darkness.

"I won't say one word to hinder you, dear, precious father," she whispered, "but, oh! I feel as if I couldn't endure it, 'tis all so sudden, and we are so happy here, so wonderfully happy and favored in everything."

Stephen Bradley held the bright head close against his breast, while his hand smoothed caressingly the brown tresses that crowned it. But his lips failed to speak the comfort his heart craved for her, and the girl cried softly while praying silently for patience and courage to endure all that might come to her in the future that seemed so suddenly to grow cloudy and somber, with the promise of a storm.

"Oh, Father," at length she said, "to have you gone, and to have to leave this dear home, all the home, the real home, I have ever known, it does seem now as though I couldn't endure it. Where shall I go, and what shall I do anywhere else?"

"You needn't leave here, if you wish to stay, my daughter," her father said.

Mary lifted her head, while a sweet smile broke through her tears.

"Will you stay at home, too? Have you changed your mind?"

"Poor darling!" her father whispered, tenderly. "I did not mean that, but I thought perhaps I could arrange in some way so that you could still remain here. Jasper Hammond came home last week discharged from the army. He is lame and must always remain so, and until he gains in strength, will find it very hard to provide a home for his wife and mother. I was thinking, as I came home, that we might take them here, and he could keep things in order and have a home, and we could thus give and receive a benefit. How would you like that?"

"How thoughtful you are, Father!" Mary answered, while her tears flowed afresh. "I shall like that way better than any other, but, Father, how soon must you go?"

"A week from tomorrow I must go to the camp for recruits, but most likely it will be some time before I shall leave there for the seat of war. I'll go and see Jasper this afternoon, and if he accepts my offer, why then, we'll have them moved here, and all settled before I go away."

Poor Mary! Through the long hours of the day, and in the still longer watches of the night, like a great weight on her heart, lay the dread of her father's departure. She was brave and patriotic, and had labored with heart and hand for the comfort of the soldiers, and was ready still to devote time and strength unlimited. Yet she was a woman, and a very loving one, and her father was almost her earthly all, and she so leaned upon him for advice and affection that the trial seemed more than she could endure, for she was both young and human.

Work didn't "go easy," and just when the day and night were clasping hands, she crept wearily into their pleasant sitting room where the rosy flush of sunset still smiled cheeringly. Throwing herself down on the sofa watched the light fade more and more, till the pictures of her parents, hanging side by side over the mantelshelf, grew dim and shadowy, and then faded entirely in the darkness. It was only the second night since her father had told her his decision, but that sad moment seemed away back in the past, and the girl felt as if she must have lived weeks since then.

"Only two nights more shall we be together by ourselves," she said, going back to her old habit of talking to herself, "and then it won't hardly seem as though I should feel glad to have people coming here to stay. I oughtn't to feel so, for I like the plan, if he must leave me, but it's so hard, oh! It's so hard! What should I do, now, if 'twasn't for the hope I have in God and His loving care? I have pitied the soldiers' families so, and now I shall share their grief and anxiety, as I never could before. How I wish everybody would do just right, and then there would be no need of fighting. Oh, dear, dear! If sin could only be all ended, and goodness reign all over the world, how blessed it would be!"

And then, as if thought took a new channel, she went on,

"I believe, though, that there is a great difference whether soldiers are fighting for the right or not. I would rather be myself, with my father going away as he is, just a common soldier, than to belong to the family of the leading general in the southern army. How I wish I could see the end, and know I should see him come home in safety. But I must leave that with God. He has helped me in many smaller troubles, He will not forsake me in this," and she slipped from the sofa, and with bowed head and bended knees, craved the help and comfort she needed.

When Mr. Bradley came home an hour later, he found the room bright and cheerful, too, ready to welcome him. She drew a low chair close beside him, as he sat down, and laid her head fondly against him.

"I believe I've got about everything arranged for your comfort, and Jasper will be a faithful friend, I feel certain." Mr. Bradley spoke encouragingly, and Mary tried to smile.

"I'm sure he will, too," she said, "I don't fear but I shall be taken care of, but I dread having you gone, and all you may have to suffer, and oh! Father, what if-if-if you should never come back again?"

"We must leave that with God, my child. I feel that this is the call of duty, and if I follow it, God will take care of me, and you know He has promised that those who trust Him shall find in Him a shield and buckler, a refuge and rock of defense. Can't you trust Him?"

"I do, dear Father, but it's so hard to lose you. You're all I have."

"I saw Alice today, Mary, and she is in trouble, too, so her father told me. I wondered what had stolen the sunshine from her eyes. He said that news had been received that William Stevens, to whom she has pledged her faith, has been severely wounded, and his father is going out to see him. Alice wishes to go also, and the doctor thinks they shall permit her to do so. She looked sad enough."

"Poor Alice! She has never known what real sorrow is. She's had the sunshiniest life of anyone I know of. It will be so sad to her, the long journey, and then to find him suffering, and oh! Father, did they say he was dangerously wounded? You didn't say so, did you?" Mary was fast forgetting her own grief in thinking of her friend's.

"I think the telegram was only to the effect that he was severely wounded, and of course the fears of his friends magnify the uncertainty. Mr. Stevens thinks he shall start tomorrow morning. Alice told me, as I met her in the hall just as I came out, to ask you to remember her. She wished to see you, but her father thought it best for her to remain at home this evening."

"Oh, how much sorrow this war does cause! Will the end ever come? It seems as though it grew worse and worse?"

"Because it comes nearer home, my darling, you have only known of its horrors as you have seen others' grief and anguish. Now it comes to you and yours, and it is proportionally harder to endure."

Slowly and yet too quickly the days passed away and the good-byes must needs be spoken. Mary was calm, but weak with that sickening faintness that comes with deep grief. Mary went wearily up stairs to her own quiet room, to lay her burden before the Lord, and renew her strength by prayer.

Once or twice, for a few brief hours, Mary saw her father, before he was ordered to the ranks, and then that life was turned over to the cruel chances of war. No, not quite that, for Mary knew that these chances and changes were subordinate to God's all wise providences. It was sweet to carry her griefs to Him and feel certain of comfort and aid.

Alice Osborne had returned widowed in heart and full of anguish. She had reached that distant hospital only to find that her heart's chosen one was fast sinking into the sleep which knows no waking. Brave and loving to the last, he had put off the soldier's armor for the victor's palm branch and the great Captain's, "Well done!" They brought home the poor, maimed body, and laid it to rest under the green sods in his native village.

Mary felt as the days wore on, that those who had "watching and waiting" at home appointed as their portion had not the last part of the burden to bear. In her friend's grief she felt so keen a sympathy, that Alice seemed to find her dearest earthly consolation in Mary's companionship.

Shedding around her the pure influence of a consistent life, and ever kindly thoughtful for the comfort and good of others, as Mary had been, it was no wonder that much sympathy was felt for her when her father's enlistment was known, and much anxiety also, lest he should never return. The whole neighborhood felt for her while Alice was by no mean overlooked. Mr. Hammond and his family proved well worthy the trust placed in them, while in return they found a pleasant home.

After five years service as teacher in the Martinsville school, Lucy Day, in consequence of the death of her mother and grandfather, the subsequent marriage of Lottie, and the permanent ill health of Susan which left the care of the household too heavy a weight upon Anna's young shoulders, much to the regret of her patrons and pupils, felt it her duty to return home. Fred had almost completed his course at the theological school. Willie was preparing for college, while John, good, practical, hard working John, was his father's right hand man, and was content with the life of a farmer, while the stores of wisdom that he was constantly garnering, rendered him no unfit companion for the best cultivated minds.

It was a bitter stroke to the whole family when the wife and mother bade them adieu. Yet their grief was solaced by the remembrance of the beautiful calm of her trusting death, a death so full of peace that it seemed indeed that she but, "shut her eyes, and entered straight, another golden chamber of the King, larger than this she left, and lovelier."

"I have been happy in my life, dear husband," so she said, "and am indeed happy in dying. Through Christ I have gained the victory over the fear of the grave, and only that I grieve to leave you and my children. I would rather go that stay."

When Grandpa Day died, they had thought the companion of so many long years must soon follow him. Her great loss seemed to bewilder her. Forgetting the living present, she lived in that far away past, when she and her John had stood at the foot of that long hill, the hill of life, which they had so patiently and lovingly climbed together, and in the freshness and strength of youthful affection joined hands for the journey.

Susan's health had never been firm, and at last it utterly failed. When Lucy went home at the close of her engagement, Susan had been confined to her room for several months with but a frail hope of ever again joining in the active duties of life. Gentle and patient, she seemed ever ready to cheer and comfort others. So much of sunshine did she contrive to scatter around her, that John used to say that Susan's room was a perfect trap to catch sunbeams, and so it came to be called the "sunbeam trap" by the whole family. Never a kind deed or pleasant scene of which the others were cognizant but reached her chamber, and somehow she contrived to smooth away difficulties and make crooked things straight in a wonderfully comforting manner.

Her room, with its picture-hung walls, its never absent bouquet in the summer time, and pots of lowering plants in the winter, its plentiful supply of books and magazines, and the many little articles that love and taste could devise to gladden the invalid, was "a sunny spot to nestle in." No one ever left it ungladdened. True, the flowers were seldom rare, and the pictures were mostly the products of Anna's pencil, but they were charming for all that, and no one ever thought of criticizing or seeking for imperfections. There, amid her books, pictures and flowers, lay the sweet, gentle invalid, often suffering extremely, but never murmuring.

"A letter from Fred, dear Mary!" and Anna's blithe face smiled in at the open door. "He's coming home tomorrow, God willing, and says he has pleasant news to impart, what do you suppose it is? It can't be that he is going to Smithville to settle, for he wrote of that to Father more than a week ago, so he wouldn't call that news."

"I don't know, little Curiosity, perhaps he's changed his mind about going to Smithville and has some more desirable call, though that doesn't seem very probable. I think he was pleased with the prospect of going there."

"Yes, indeed he was, and he writes in Father's letter about the parsonage. Agnes and he were coming here the week before his ordination, you know we read that the other day. Just at the close of this letter, he says, if it will please you, he will be married at home, and in your room, so that we can all be around him. Agnes has no home, and has been staying with some distant relatives since she finished teaching. He says Aggy proposed this plan in preference to a more public wedding, and because, too, she wanted to please you."

"A new sister to love!" said Susan, in her low, sweet tones. "I hope her life may be a long and happy one. I am sure it deserves to be."

"Fred will try to make it so, I'm sure, and for one, I love her dearly already, and mean to make her love me as well, but what are you thinking about, Susan? Are you curious about Fred's news, too?"

"I wasn't thinking of that Anna. I was only looking back over the past six years since we came here, and thinking of all the changes since that day when we first gathered beneath this roof and said, 'This is our home.' How proud and rebellious we felt, you not so much as we older ones, and how Fred, called home from college declared he would get an education in spite of everything, and do something of mark in the world, so that he should be famous, and through him, the rest of us.

"I remember how Lottie and I encouraged him, and how Mother smiled on us sadly, while John said he'd hoe a broad row yet, and we girls would shine in the highest ranks of the cultivated society in the land. 'You shall have your rights, girls,' he used to say, and how often he used to add, 'Yes, the king shall have his ain again.'"

"I can remember how he used to say that, and how Father called some of his projects, 'Castles in Spain,' and I used to wonder what that meant."

"Then how differently we all felt," Susan continued, "when we learned to love Jesus. The boys still desired to study, but their aims were so different, and subservient to the great object of doing God's service, and making their own lives and those around them better for their having lived. I don't think one of us has cared to be prosperous because we could show the world the fact, but only for the good and the beauty and the joy with which we could enrich our home and our lives, and the service we could render God and humanity thereby."

"Was you ever proud, Susan? Did you long for money that you might make a display like Laura Howard and all the rest of that set?"

"I am afraid I did, and for no better reason. Only when I learned to love God and know the worth of religion, I felt very differently. Why, in those days I should have made myself and everybody else miserable if I had been obliged to lie on a sick bed as I do now. The very idea of one of my brothers settling down as a country minister would have seemed almost a disgrace, and for John to be a farmer, why, 'twould have been beyond endurance. Now how glad we feel for and about Fred, and as for John, who would ask for a better and happier brother than he is? And think of the good he is able to do!"

"We are very happy, but, Susan, I do wish Mother could have lived a few years longer," Anna said.

The sick girl answered, "We can never cease to lament our loss, but even in this we can, if we will, discern mercy. God spared us all till, from out the darkness of unbelief, we had been led, a united family, into the light of the truth as it is in Jesus. Then till we were all established and grounded in the faith, and with the ways of life plainly defined before us, and then he called her up higher, that we might learn still more surely how our joys were His gifts, and could be at anytime recalled, as best pleased His wisdom. Her life, even in her worldliness, was a very unselfish one, and after she found peace in believing, she added the Christian graces to her natural loveliness of character, and the last memories of her life, and those of her happy death, are legacies of abiding richness to us all."

Anna was weeping softly, and when Lucy came in shortly after, and looked in questioning silence for the cause of her grief, she looked up with a faint smile as she explained,

"I believe I've been looking for griefs, but Susan counts her blessings. Don't look so sorrowful Lucy, 'tis nothing new, only I got into the shadows, and even Susan could not scatter them all. My eyes are so dim that I require a good deal of sunshine."

"I've just heard some sorrowful news." Lucy looked exceedingly pained, and Anna half-frightened, while Susan's lips moved as if in prayer. "It doesn't concern us immediately, but in the light of past friendships it seems a grief to me. Don't you remember how much everybody thought of Laura Howard's husband and how, last spring, when they were married, there was so much said and written about the wedding, and the fine beginning of the young couple, of their beautiful home, and all that? There were some who wondered how, with no acknowledged business, he could support so much style, but most of our people believed him wealthy enough to live without labor, or perhaps I ought to say, without business of any kind. The truth has come sadly out, he was a professional gambler, and indulged in the very worst vices known. Last week he was killed in a duel and Laura is terribly sick, raving in the delirium of fever, and seemingly near to death. Think how they have lived, and now to die and have no time for preparation! Harry was engaged in the same quarrel, and was obliged to flee to escape the clutches of the law. Mr. Howard and his wife have gone on to New York. John has just reached home, and he saw them yesterday on their way. Mrs. Howard seemed almost beside herself with grief, while her husband looked as though many years had been added to his age. John said he hadn't seen a sadder picture of grief for years."

"Poor Laura!" came from Anna's tender heart.

"Poor parents!" Susan said, "but," she added, as though sure of her source of strength and confidence, "we can leave them all with God. He can lighten their burden and give them consolation."

John caught the trusting words as he entered, and stooping over to kiss his sister, said tenderly, "They need His presence, but they are far from possessing it now. Mr. Howard seemed like an insane person. I heard him say to a friend, that he didn't see what he had ever done to have so much trouble come all in a heap, just when he had begun to see his way clear, and was thinking of retiring from business, and taking comfort in his old age. It was splendid misery, I assure you girls, and it made my heart ache with pity and sorrow."

"They thought Laura was past the hope of recovering?" queried Anna.

"That was the imply of the telegram. Still, I think the poor parents buoyed themselves up with the hope that she might be spared."

Lucy rose softly and went out of the room, all the way down stairs, and while she was spreading the table for tea, her heart was full of thoughts of her early friend. All intercourse between the two had long ago ceased. Lucy had learned of more than one unkind and unjust remark that Laura had made concerning her. She thought about the offer made her years previous and also of the difference that an opposite decision might have made in her whole life. She too, might have taken a false step and found, as Laura had now, her life blighted by the premature crushing of woman's sweetest hopes of earthly happiness. How kindly her step had been guided! How tenderly her griefs had been apportioned! And with what sweet consolations had she been comforted! She sang, as if to renew her trust in the Holy One, on whom her soul relied.

"I wish poor Howard had this confidence in God's wisdom, and accepted all as coming in His wise providence," Mr. Day said sadly, " 'tis a hard lesson for one as old as he is to learn. Youth is the easier time, before the heart gets too deeply encrusted with worldliness. How often have I regretted the long years I spent blindly following my own conceits, and trying vainly to satisfy myself with the fruits, which they brought me. It will be a blessed thing for my poor friends if this great stroke brings them to God."

"I wonder what Harry has been guilty of. He was in a law office, wasn't he?" asked Lucy.

"So I have understood," her father answered, "but 'tis reported that he has spent more time recently in gambling hells, and driving fast horses, than he has in study. The lawyer, with whom he has been reading has threatened several times to expel him from the office, his conduct has been so scandalous, only his father's wealth had held him up for some time past.

"I believe the quarrel which resulted in the duel commenced one evening in a gambling saloon, and one thing led on to another, till a challenge was given and accepted. Laura's husband, Lewis Burton fell, mortally wounded. Harry was so beside himself with rage and the whiskey they had fortified themselves with, that he stabbed Burton's rival, and, as his life was despaired of, Harry was advised to flee. Detectives have been put on his track, so the paper's state, for heavy forgeries are laid to his charge. Indeed, a rumor has been started that his father must suffer largely by his crime, perhaps find himself ruined as a man of business."

"I heard that spoken of several times, yesterday and today," said John, "and each time with more certainty. To be bereft of children and home, perhaps at one fell stroke, will seem a heavy blow to the proud but only doting hearts of the lonely couple. I pitied them when I saw their anguish, from the very bottom of my heart." Then the conversation turned to other subjects, Fred's approaching marriage, and his settlement as minister, were discussed at length, with many suggestions for the comfort and pleasure of the young couple.

So the days, as fair with loving deeds, kindly words and earnest prayers as a summer meadow is sweet and lovely with clover blossoms, wore on, till one pleasant September afternoon found the whole family gathered in Susan's room, pleasanter than usual with its profuse decorations of vines and flowers.

Agnes Stafford made a lovely bride, and when the few words had been spoken which joined her fate with that of the young minister, and the father's blessing had been craved, many a welcoming word told how gladly she was received in to the family circle. Susan's sweet face smiled up from her pillows, while the aged grandmother seemed living over again her own bridal experiences. She told the young people, as they grouped around her, that her John was a good son, she doubted not he would prove as good a husband, at any rate she was not afraid to trust him. It was a cheerful day for a wedding, the sun burst out with a clear prophecy, if the old saying may be trusted, "Happy the bride that the sun shines on." So the old lady talked on, and believed herself in the springtime of her life's blessedness.

Two days later, the same train that bore Fred Day and his bride, with Lucy and their father, to this field of labor, where the servant of God was to be publicly consecrated to his Master's service, brought back the lifeless remains of Laura Burton with those of her wretched husband. Together they were laid to rest in the family tomb. She had awaked to consciousness a few brief hours before her death, and begged, as a last request; to be carried home for burial, and that her husband might be laid beside her. The wretched parents had promised in the great grief to comply with her wishes.

Lucy Day sat with bowed head and fast falling tears as the swift wheels rolled on, her heart was deeply pained at this terrible fate of her early friend. Prayerless her life had been, and as far as she knew, it had ended prayerlessly. It seemed to Lucy that on everything "too late" looked forth piteously, as though calling for tears and impressing the lesson of duty. She said to herself,

"Oh, that Laura could have learned the joy there is in believing, the peace that comes of resting on the help on One mighty to save. Who never turns away from a pleading cry, or a prayer for guidance and protection, but whose mercy is unspeakable, and past finding out!"

She almost blamed herself for not having, in some way, striven to interest Laura in sacred things, perhaps she might have given heed to her, had she persevered in her efforts. But now she had passed away from the reach of all efforts for her salvation. All through yearning for a now unattainable privilege swept sadly across her mind, and she only grew calm when she rested back on the promise. "Acquaint now thyself with him, and be at peace, thereby good shall come unto thee." She must leave what she could not help with God. How many times Susan had spoken words like these in her weak, sweet tones, and she felt a new determination to labor faithfully for those around, that her skirts might be pure from the blood of souls.

Then she thought how strangely God ordains circumstances to bear on the hearts of the children of men, and marked the blending of a calm trust and a rapturous rejoicing that lighted the fine face of a young man seated near her. Of whom the "good news" of which Fred had written had been told during her brother's stay at home. Justin Rand had arrived to attend the wedding ceremony of Fred and Agnes.

Through all his college life Justin Rand had been a dear friend of Fred, and as the theological school that Fred had attended was in the same place where Justin was reading law and where he had afterwards entered on the practice of his profession, the intimacy had continued. Blending fine conversational powers with a winning address and a rich fund of acquired knowledge, the young man was a great favorite with a very wide circle of friends. There was just one thing that saddened Fred's feelings toward him. Though outwardly respectful, he made no scruple of affirming his utter and complete disbelief in the Bible, and declared it all a wonderfully plausible story, gotten up with consummate skill, having a strange charm for romantic minds, and for those seeking some species of comfort for suffering or grief.

Many had been the long argument in which Fred had tried to convince him of the truth as it is in Jesus, but all had seemed in vain. "It's of no use," Justin would answer. "I admire your trusting confidence Fred, but don't expect me to share it. I don't believe, and you do, and here we must be content to let the matter rest." Often and often had prayers been offered for the blinded young man, who, so lovely and upright in his daily life, yet lacked the one thing needful. At the home of the Days he had been a pleasant visitor, and much interest was felt in his spiritual welfare.

A few weeks before Fred returned home, Justin had accompanied him to a small village where he was to preach. He had been more than ever fervent in his opposition to the story of the cross, asserting that he could preach himself, if he could only have a chance.

During the service of the Sabbath school, what was Fred's dismay at seeing his friend get up, at an invitation of the superintendent of the school, to address the scholars. He stepped forward with his usual ease, and moved his lips to speak, but no sound broke the stillness, and a dead gloom overspread his face. For more than a minute, it seemed many minutes to the waiting company, he stood there as silent as a statue, and then sank into a seat near and buried his face in his hands. With a quickly beating heart, Fred approached him, and refusing the proffered assistance of several kindly souls present, he hurried his friend from the room.

"What is it, Justin?" he ask anxiously. "Of what were you thinking?"

"I don't know what influenced me, I only know that, like Saul of Tarsus, I found it hard to kick against the pricks. My impious attempt at scorning the Christian's sacred right to speak for his Master, has ended in my eyes being opened to a sense of my own wretched blindness and unpardonable sinfulness before God. I believe it all now! I haven't one doubt left, it all came to me like a flash, but I don't think it can do me any good, only to increase my misery."

The young man had spoken as though impelled by a resistless conviction of the truth of which he was speaking. The words last uttered were inexpressible sad, and Fred, looking to the fountain of all consolation, said only, "God so loved the world, that he gave His only begotten Son, that whosoever believeth in him should not perish but have eternal life."

"That may do for others, but it can't mean such as me, my condemnation is certain," was the answer.

Still the young preacher's voice dropped pearls of truth. "God sent not His Son into the world to condemn the world, but that the world through Him might be saved. This is his commandment, That we should believe on the name of His Son, Jesus Christ, and love one another."

"I do believe! I do believe!" he reiterated again and again, "but it's of no use, believing only makes my guilt seem more terrible, but it won't save me."

"It saved Saul of Tarsus, and it saved the thief on the cross." Justin was silent, and Fred went on, "You show that you don't really believe, if you thus doubt Christ's power to save you. He is an all powerful and a universal Saviour, offering the blessings of salvation freely to all, and to refuse to accept this, personally, while believing it ample for others, shows a willful doubt of His power. Throw yourself entirely on His mercy and trust Him freely, and He will pardon freely, and your darkness will gleam with the brightness of noontide splendor."

That pride was crushed, and held subservient to a desire to know the truth, was evident from the young man's manner when he resumed his place among the worshipers in the afternoon. His tear filled eyes and lips that quivered with suppressed feeling, told how some of the searching truths presented, touched his inmost feelings.

"Who will believe me if I tell of faith in God?" he said abruptly, as they were walking after the services of the afternoon. "I have made no secret of my peculiar notions, and have even boasted, impious wretch that I was, of the utter impossibility of such fables having any influence over my mind. Now I haven't a doubt of the truth of the word of salvation, and the story of Christ's life and death, but I might as well not believe, for no one will have any faith in me."

"That's a temptation of the spirit of evil. Such feelings are snares such as he loves to spread for unwary feet. If God sees your sincerity, what need you care whether your fellow mortals read your motives aright or not?"

"It will be wonderful mercy, if Christ saves me. Only think how I have abused and reviled him! If I could once have the assurance that he had indeed forgiven and accepted me. I feel now as though there would be nothing but I could suffer and accomplish for His sake."

"Don't you believe He is able?"

"I believe He is God, blessed and all powerful."

"Do you doubt His willingness to save?"

"I can't say that I do, else why did He suffer and die at all?"

"Where, then, do you find room for these hesitating doubts, and this unwillingness to leave yourself and all your interests, for time and eternity, in His hands?"

"I don't think I am unwilling, only it seems too much for me to hope for."

"Have you prayed over it?"

"I have followed, and joined in your prayers."

"I think I see the trouble now, Justin, you have not asked for this great blessing. You are willing to receive it, but not from your bended knees do you look up and say, with strong cryings, Have mercy on me, O Lord, the chief of sinners."

"I never prayed in my life, I used to say my prayers, when I was a child, but only because my mother told me to. I never felt the force of them, or thought them of much consequence, any way."

"God' Word tells us, 'He that covereth His sins shall not prosper, but whoso confesseth and forsaketh them, shall find mercy.' Again we find the promise, 'If any of you lack wisdom, let him ask of God, that giveth to all men liberally, and upbraideth not, and it shall be given him. But let him ask in faith, nothing wavering.'"

In the earnestness of their conversation they had passed on out of the village, and were now treading the shaded footpath, leading beneath branches of forest trees, the boughs fast putting on the gorgeous drapery of autumn. As they reached a quiet, sheltered knoll, where the moss grown trunk of a fallen tree furnished an inviting resting place, Justin sank down beside it, saying, "The forests are often called, 'God's temples,' I will make this spot my altar of petition, and lift my heart and voice in my first prayer."

Fred knelt beside him, and as the faltering accents of the earnest seeker after peace fell on the listener's ears, he almost doubted his sense of hearing. His inmost soul rejoiced over the fulfillment of the promise given of old, "Call unto me and I will answer thee, and show thee great and might things that thou knowest not." Many prayers had been offered for Justin Rand, and now the answer was coming, the "great and mighty thing," the conversion of an immortal soul.

As the waters flow from a fountain, suddenly broken up, so from the young lawyer's "broken and contrite heart," the cry went forth and up into the heavenly city, and there was joy among the angels of God over another repenting sinner.

When Justin ceased his prayer, Fred followed in simple but earnest pleadings. As they arose from their knees, Justin lifted a face radiant with happiness toward his friend. While the words trembled on his lips, "I *know* in whom I have believed,' yes, I *know*, not by hearing merely, not by a general belief, but I *know* Him as mine. He has come into my heart. I feel all the truth of your afternoon text, 'Being justified by faith, we have peace with God through our Lord Jesus Christ. By whom also we have access by faith into this grace wherein we stand, and rejoice in hope of the glory of God."

"Your doubts are all fled?" asked Fred.

"All gone! I feel like a new creature! It is all so plain, so wonderfully clear and complete now, I wonder at my long blindness. Think how much time I have lost that might have been used in God's service. Think of all my past opportunities for doing good, passed by unheeded, and worse than unheeded, used for wrong purposes. Henceforth I am the Lord's, and life, strength, talents and education, all I have, shall be used in His service. I don't know how I have ever lived so long without this blessed hope."

From that hour he had unfalteringly rested on God, and prayerful consideration only fixed more firmly his first impulsive resolve, or what might more truly perhaps he called the directions he seemed to read on the first page of his new found rules for life, "Go preach my gospel." He had already completed his arrangements to enter on a course of preparation for the ministry. Called of God he felt himself to be, and when someone, lukewarm and faltering in faith, had spoken of his sacrifices and the "great cross" it must be to give up such a splendid prospect for worldly honor and distinction.

He had answered, with a flashing smile on his manly countenance, "A cross and a sacrifice do you call it? Rather say a glory and an honor beyond the power of this world to bestow. It is no cross for me to tell of Jesus and his pardoning mercy, no cross, but a privilege blessed beyond the power of words to tell. Think of his calling me, me in all my wickedness, and taking me out of all my wretched blindness, and the darkness where I was wandering, and lifting me, through so much love, into his marvelous light, and biding me speak for Him. Never call it a cross again, 'tis a joy and a blessing."

Truly this was "good tidings," and it brought gladness and rejoicing to the hearts that loved him. As Lucy Day thought on the wonderful dealings of God while she watched the new expression of chastened peacefulness that over spread his face, she felt that they indeed are "blessed whose iniquities are forgiven and whose sins are covered."

The hallowing influence of the day's services was felt by many hearts, and through the following winter and spring, Fred, the newly ordained servant, of the Most High was privileged in being allowed to welcome a large number of new born souls into the fellowship of the saints below, while Justin Rand was "standing up for Jesus," in life and in word, and pressing on for a more perfect understanding of his Master's will. At the home of the Days, the homeliest every day duties were lovingly performed, as in Jesus' name, and were hallowed by prayer and praise.

With the opening spring, a time of severe suffering came to Susan, but the everlasting arms, on which she trustingly leaned, held her up, and patience was beautifully exemplified in her daily life, with its clinging pains and terrible burdens.

On the Howard family a sudden blight seemed to fall. A thorough investigation showed how wide spread had been the villainy of both Harry and his sister's husband. In various ways Mr. Howard's kindness had been so imposed upon, his blind partiality so abused, that ruin, swift and sudden, stared him in the face. With his cruel losses by death, and by the false dealing of those he has so trusted, came the loss of ambition. When at mid winter, his home and its luxurious appointments were sold under the hammer of the auctioneer, he sank into a state of imbecility sad to witness.

Mrs. Howard never rallied from the shock of her daughter's death, and before the New Year came, just when homes were fair with Christmas wreaths and pleasant with Christmas rejoicing, she closed her eyes on earth forever. Many days of her long illness were cheered by Lucy Day's presence, and just at the last, it seemed as though a hope, faint as the pulse beat of the dying woman, shed its comfort over her closing hours on earth. With a last weak pressure of her icy hand, at Lucy's low spoken, "Can you leave yourself entirely in Jesus' hands?" her soul went out into the unknown mysteries of eternity.

Hardened in his grief, Mr. Howard yielded to no softening influence. It seemed to those who pitied him so tenderly, that he had sinned away the day of grace, and that the Spirit had taken its leave of him forever. When, his family and wealth all gone, his mind in a measure gone too, and a perfect wreck, he wandered hither and thither, of him might it truly have been said, "For thus saith the Lord, Thy bruise is incurable, and thy wound is grievous. There is none to plead thy cause that thou mayst be bound up; thou hast no healing medicines. Why criest thou for thine affliction? Thy sorrow is incurable for the multitude of thine iniquity, because thy sins were increased, I have done these things unto thee."

There were those who offered him the shelter of a home, but he was best suited to wander according to his own fancies, and few would have recognized in the wretched looking vagabond, the once proud and successful man of business.

Mr. Day pleaded with him to remain with them. Except the poor man, dead while yet living scorned the kind offer with the impious words, "You have too much psalm singing and praying at your house for me. I've no taste for such things. I won't be beholden to such, as you, who will think your granting me favors, will give you the right to be everlastingly preaching your religion. I don't believe in it, and I won't listen to it." He had willfully led his wife, through her love for him, away from the right, and over him hung the fearful saying, "Woe unto him by whom the offense cometh."

Chapter XII
Toiling for the Brave

Mary Bradley's room was filled with busy workers. Here a group of young women pulling or scraping lint, there, others rolling bandages, while the gleam of knitting needles and the stitch on stitch who were sewing, blended in the lengthening web of conversation, filling the air with the music of pleasant sounds.

"There must be a note in every 'Comfort Bag.' Cousin Will says the soldiers look for them the very first thing," so said one of the workers.

While another added, with a curl of her lips, "I hope none of these things will fall into the hands of the rebels."

"So do I," was echoed again and again.

But Mary Bradley said, "I'm sure theses bags, with their letters full of Bible truth, would do much good among our foes. You mustn't write anything, girls, that you can't ask God's blessing to rest upon, and a rebel's soul is just as precious as any other."

"That's true, Mary, but still I can't at all like the idea of having anything we do for our own soldiers, benefit those who are fighting against them. Perhaps, though, if they were led to repent, they would see the wrong they are doing, and, in returning to God, return to their allegiance to their country. There are twenty-four bags and nearly an equal number of letters ready to go in them. Won't it be a good idea to have the letters read for the evening's entertainment? It will be something new, and for my part

I think I should like it much." Mabel Grant's proposal was received with favor, and having chosen one for the post of reader, silence was enjoined, and the reading commenced.

Patriotic and full of Christian earnestness, there was not one among the letters but would speak words of comfort and encouragement to those for whom they were intended, while one or two were merely copies of some sweet poet's fancies, wherein one soul speaks forth the feelings of multitudes.

One poem, it was decided, should be placed with a pair of socks, as the most appropriate way of sending it. It was called, "Socks for the feet of the brave and true," and was highly praised.

"Where did you find that gem, Lizzie Dunn? You seem to have a ability of getting many sweet little scraps of poetry that no one else among us happens to find."

"I found these in one of Mr. Dunn's 'Tracts for our Army and Navy,' and I have since heard a pretty story about them. It seems that the author is a young female schoolteacher, and that the poem originated in something like this. A dialogue was being prepared for a school exhibition, and the various ways in which the cause of our country might be helped were brought forward, when among others, the question was asked, 'What can woman do?' Of course there are many things she can do to aid and cheer, but the answer came in part, in this poem."

"Read it again, Leonard," came in a chorus, and again the melody of the reader's voice joined with the written words,

> "Click, click, click! How the needles go,
> Through the busy fingers to and fro!
>
> With no bright colors of Berlin wool,
> Delicate hands today are full
>
> Only a yarn of deep, dull blue,
> Socks for the feet of the brave and true.

Yet click, click! How the needles go!
'Tis a power within that nerves them so.

Maiden, mother, and grandma sit,
Earnest and thoughtful while they knit.

Many the silent prayers they pray,
Many the teardrops brushed away,

While busily on the needles go,
Widen and narrow, heel and toe.

The grandma thinks, with a thrill of pride,
How her mother knit, and spun beside,

For that patriot band, in olden days,
Who died the 'Stars and Stripes' to raise?

Now she in turn knits for the brave
Who'd die that glorious flag to save?

She is glad, she says, 'the boys' have gone
'Tis just what their grandfathers would have done,

But she heaves a sigh, and the tears will start,
For 'the boys' were the pride of the grandma's heart.

The mother's look is calm and high
God only knows her soul's deep cry!

In Freedom's name, at Freedom's call,
She gave her son-in them, her all.

The maiden's cheek wears a paler shade,
But the light in her eye is undismayed,

Faith and Hope give strength to her sight,
She sees a red dawn after the night.

Oh, soldiers, brave, will it brighten the day,
And shorten the march on the weary way,

To know that at home the loving and true
Are knitting, and hoping, and praying for you?

Soft are their voices when speaking your name,
Proud are the glories when hearing your fame,

And the gladdest hour in their lives will be
When they greet you after the victory."

"The second hearing discloses new beauties, that must go with a pair of Grandma Brewer's socks, and let's have a cheering poem, or a comforting passage from the Bible put with each pair. It won't be much trouble, and who can tell how many weary hours may be brightened thereby?" suggested Mary.

"Always on the look out for doing good to somebody, Mary," and Dr. Osborne's dark eyes smiled into those of the girl, who regarded him almost in the light of a second father. "You make your religion shine out in little things, and that's the kind I wish was more current among the mass of professing Christians. Here's a sunbeam for you, in the shape of a letter from your father."

How glad the welcome which the letter received from the loving daughter, the light of her expressive eyes, and the deepened color glowing on her cheek, gave ample token. She would have laid it aside to mingle with her guests and share their tasks of love, but the doctor called after her,

"I prescribe that you go and sit down in that corner, and read your letter, after that I have a story to tell you."

With a quick glance of thankfulness, Mary obeyed, while Dr. Osborne took his seat among the bandage rollers, and was soon busily at work.

"Oh, how dreadful!" the words came with a quick gasp from Mary's lips, and to the looks of inquiry turned upon her, she answered, "Father's account of the last battle is so terrible! There was an unusual number badly wounded, and the supplies have been cut off, so there is great suffering. Efforts were making to get comforts for the poor fellows, but in the face of many difficulties."

"How I wish we could send these things there!" said one of the girls, "but, after all, it is so little that we can do in the way of relieving the sick and wounded, I don't feel at all contented. I want to do so much, and yet do so little."

"It isn't so much the largeness of the deed accomplished, as the motive that leads to its doing, that God looks at. If we do all we can, and the best we can, 'tis all that can be expected of us," said Pastor Adams.

"But there's so much to be done," the girl said, "and even our greatest efforts look so small when placed in the balance against what is needed."

" 'Tis the patient doing of little that in the end amounts to much. I don't wonder at your anxiety and your desire to do a great deal, it is perfectly natural, but you must not let this feeling of discontent at the little you can do, cheat you of satisfaction at being enabled to do even that," continued Pastor Adams.

"Now and then," said the doctor, "there comes an opportunity for some great deed of self-sacrifice for the good of others, or for the cause of right, and the story I promised to relate is an instance of this kind. I think most of you will remember the young farmer, Lyman Raymond, who buried his wife and child some more than a year ago, and soon afterwards enlisted. I received a letter from his captain this morning, which contained an account of his heroic death.

"The regiment to which he belonged had been at the front but a few weeks, and on Monday of last week they took part in that same severe conflict of which Mary's father writes. Our troops were driven back, and many dead were left on the field, mid way between the opposing ranks, while most of the wounded were carried back in the retreat, which was after all, little less than a triumph, as was afterwards proved.

"But there was one man, left on the field, unable to walk in consequence of wounds, and yet alive and eagerly watching for aid, as they could plainly see through a field glass. The question arose, 'Who will try to save him?' He was a general favorite, and the only son of a widowed mother, whose life was bound up in his. There were many brave men in the ranks, who had stood unflinchingly the chance shots that might any moment bring death to them. Yet his seemed so sure a seeking death that it is no wonder if the thought of home and loved one, the thought, too, that they themselves might so soon lie cold in death, or be left at the mercy of cruel foes, kept them from venturing.

Just when it seemed certain that no aid would be forthcoming for the wounded man, Lyman Raymond stepped forward. Simply saying, "I have neither wife nor child to grieve for me, pray God to be with me, and, if it must be that I fall, to take me to Himself, pray one and all, comrades,' he then started on his perilous mission. The captain wrote that more than half the company to which Raymond belonged fell on their knees, and what was most touching of all, he heard the little drummer boy saying in sobbing tones, 'Now I lay me down to sleep.'

Anxious eyes watched the poor fellow as he went steadily forward, and the balls seemed to whistle harmlessly around him. Lifting his suffering comrade, he came back more slowly, but steadily still, and all believed that not one of the whizzing bullets had brought him harm. When they grouped around him, more than one stout heart was filled with grief at the pallor and agony that over spread his face. Laying down tenderly the comrade whose life he had saved, he said faintly, 'I may have saved your life, but I have lost my own,' and sank back into the arms that were outstretched to uphold him. He had been terribly wounded in going out, but with wonderful self-control he persevered till his deed of mercy was accomplished. As tenderly as possible he was cared for, but just at sunset he received the summons, 'Come up higher,' and with a calm and happy trust, his spirit returned to God who gave it."

"And the comrade for whom he gave his life?" asked Alice, her beautiful eyes full of tears.

"He is in a fair way of recovering, so the captain wrote."

"I think that the articles finished had better be packed and started immediately," interrupted Pastor Adams. "I expect a young friend at my house tomorrow who goes out under the patronage of the Christian Commission, and if it so please you he will gladly, I am sure, take charge of them and thus they may earlier reach their destined field."

"That is a good plan, but I wish we might finish more of the things than we can possibly tonight," Mrs. Osborne said.

Mary's quick "Come again tomorrow, all of you, the things are all here, and it will be no trouble, only a pleasure to me," met with general approval, and so the matter was arranged.

During the year that her father had been in the army, she had scarcely allowed herself leisure for needed recreation. The yearning wistfulness that spoke in each utterance of her voice, and looked out from her earnest eyes, told how her father's absence, and the knowledge of the fatigues and dangers, to which he was subjected, wore on her heart. Her Christ like unselfishness was shown in her endeavors to forget her own trials by helping others to bear their burdens.

The following evening Pastor Adams said, "Miss Bradley, allow me to introduce to you another laborer in our common cause, Brother Rand, of whom I spoke last night."

Pastor Adams had come to the Aid Meeting accompanied by his friend, whom we may recognize as the young lawyer whose singular conversion resulted in his consecrating himself to his Master's service in the ministry, with singleness of heart and earnestness of purpose.

Mary acknowledged the introduction, and then added, "I almost envy you, Mr. Rand, your privilege of ministering personally to our soldiers' comfort. If my father would only give me permission, I would like to go out and care for some of those sufferers, myself."

"We each have our mission, my dear young lady," the minister said, "yours may lie at home. You can find plenty to do here, can't you?"

"Oh, yes, sir, it comes to me in abundance."

"And what doesn't come, she hunts up," said Katie Adams. "She's as busy as a bee all the time."

"Tell Miss Bradley about that invalid lady who has done so much," said Katie.

"That I will do with pleasure," he returned.

While Mary said, as usual thinking of others' pleasure, "Perhaps the rest would like to hear, also," and so while busy fingers plied the needles, he told his story.

"The lady's name is Day, Susan Day, and for several years she has been confined to her bed with an incurable disease. She is one of the happiest Christians I ever met, and so constantly cheerful that her family calls her room the 'Sunbeam-trap.'

"When the war first broke out, and societies were organized for the relief and comfort of the soldiers, she desired to use her feeble strength to aid in this work of love. From that time till the present, when not suffering too severely to allow of it, she has devoted herself to whatever came within the scope of her ability. A large number of pairs of socks have been sent, each with a comforting sentence, or with gentle words full of pleading earnestness, written by her hand, and addressed to the receiver of the socks. More than once she has been encouraged by the reception of letters thanking her for her interest in the spiritual welfare of the soldiers.

In two instances, at least, it has proved that her 'few words' have been 'the nail in a sure place,' that has led a soul to God. Of late she has been making 'comfort bags,' very much like those on yonder table. I was much interested in her history of a 'comfort bag' that had been returned to her, after its mission had been performed. It was faded and despoiled of most of its contents, but was valued highly by its present possessor.

A lady friend of Miss Day, who was a nurse in a southern hospital, had in her ward a young soldier from the West. He was stalwart and brave fellow, but whose life was fast ebbing away through one of those terrible wounds which so soon sap the very fountain of life. One day, while attending to his wants, she found this bag under his pillow, where she had noticed that the man in sleep usually kept his only remaining hand, as though fearful of losing some cherished treasure.

"A faint smile played around the sufferer's lips as he saw the nurse noticed his carefully kept gift. He said, 'I don't know but you'll laugh at me, but that bag is the dearest possession I have just at present, and the name of the stranger lady who made it, has a large place in my memory. There is a letter in the bag, and I thank God every day that it was penned, for I believe that letter was the means of saving my soul. Perhaps you would like to read it.'

"The nurse opened the bag, and at the close of the sweet, womanly letter, so rich in the simplest and yet mightiest of gospel truths, she saw Susan Day's name. The suffering soldier showed great pleasure when she told him that the writer of the note was a dear personal friend of her own. Over and over again she had to tell him the story of Susan Day's life of patient endurance often amid severe anguish. While he in turn told how that letter had found him reckless and defiant, almost cursing God for a sudden grief that had marred his hopes, and sent him into the army. Careless of what his fate might be, and how the gentleness and purity of that letter, and the thought that women, noble and devoted as he felt the writer of that must be, were praying for such as he, and denying themselves for the sake of doing good, made him desire a purer life. How, amid long and weary marches, and when on duty in camp and field, these thoughts had been his constant companion, till at last peace had come to him through faith in Jesus, and he had enrolled himself a soldier for Christ as well as for his country.

"There was no date or residence mentioned in the letter, and therefore he had no clue to the writer, beyond the name, 'Susan Day,' and he had never supposed that his wish, sometime to know more of her, would be gratified. He wanted to thank her, so he often said, for the good she had done him, and when he died he would like to have that bag sent back to her, with the request that she would always keep it. Plus always remember, too, that even our slightest efforts for good, even if done amid great weakness, may be rich in blessings to others.

"Beside his couch of suffering a letter was written to Miss Day, and when just a day before he died, her answer was received, his gladness was touching to behold. His death had been one of triumph, and when the nurse came north, the bag had been brought back to its maker. Susan Day found it a source of comfort and encouragement. I said," continued the young minister, "that Miss Day told me the story herself. I should have said, in part, for much of it I heard from the lips of the nurse. The lady very justly remarked that eternity would alone reveal the good done by the efforts of Susan and of other women like her.

Bro. Rand glanced at the bags which a group of busy workers were filling with appropriate contents, "I hope that you have written letters for those bags full with the blessed truths of religion, and that they may be instrumental of great good. I have here," unfolding a letter as he spoke, " a letter written by a little girl in New York, and sent with a comfort bag, made by her own hands, and filled with various articles purchased by her own labors. The soldier who permitted me to retain it in my possession for a while, told me that he knew, beyond a doubt, of six who had been led to the Saviour through the influence, more or less direct, of that child's letter. Shall I read it while your work goes on?"

"By all means," said several.

The power and passion of the young man's tones gave special effect to the child's beautiful letter. It read thus:

> "Dear Soldier, I have made this bag myself, and if you see any big stitches, you must overlook them, for I am only a very little girl, eight years old last birthday. All these things I earned myself, taking care of Mrs. Gray's chickens, every night and morning, and mother said I might make as many bags as I could fill with

things, so I've made four, and this is one of them. I hope you will have a nice time using the things, even better than I have had making and getting them filled.

My grandpa is a minister, and he says that the bravest and best soldiers are those who love God best, because they won't have anything to fear if they do die, for they are sure God will let them have one of the homes that Jesus Christ has gone to get ready for the people who love Him, and try to honor Him.

"Dear Soldier, are you one of Christ's soldiers? I do so hope you are, but maybe you have never had as good a grandpa as I have, to tell you how you can be saved. He says if we are sorry for our sins, and I don't see how we can help feeling sorry for being naughty, do you? We must go to God by prayer, and tell Him how bad and sorry we feel, and ask Him to forgive us for His Son's sake, our dear Saviour, who was killed by wicked men so many years ago, and who on the cross suffered for everybody's sins. And then when God sees how sorry we are, He will send such a happy feeling, and make us sure that our sins are all blotted out by Jesus' blood. But we can't do anything just of ourselves that will make our souls safe, we've got to just repent, and believe in Jesus, and leave the rest to Him, and then afterwards try to do all as He wants to have us.

"I have written a very long letter, but I do so want you should know all about Jesus, and I want you should learn to love Him very dearly. I hope you won't get sick or wounded, and so make your little girls feel as bad as I did when my papa came home with one foot shot off, but that you will be kept safe, and live to come home. My papa has got well, now, and has gone to take care of sick soldiers in a great hospital in Washington, and we hope that he is doing lots of good. Good bye, Soldier, and don't forget what I said about Jesus, and how you can be saved. I am your little friend,

Katie Lee

Many eyes glistened with tears before the reader paused, and Pastor Adams exclaimed, "Surely it is often true, that out of the mouth of babes praise is indeed perfected."

"The very men," continued Bro. Rand, "who would have listened unmoved to a sermon by our most eloquent divines, found in the childlike simplicity and love displayed in a letter like this, the arrow of conviction that, piercing their inmost hearts, left them no peace till they found it in Jesus."

"I hope my letter will do some soldier good," said a little girl who sat near.

"I hope so too, my child," answered the minister. "You can pray that it may."

At the close of the evening the articles completed were packed, and the next morning were started on their mission, consecrated by many prayers and enriched beyond worldly calculation by the kind words and desires that had been breathed over them.

Chapter XIII
Reaping the Harvest

One bright afternoon in May, Mary Bradley sat busily sewing at an open window, through which drifted the fragrance of the apple blossoms, that made the old trees just outside look as though laden with dozens on dozens of nosegays, pink and white, and sweet as only apple blossoms are sweet. Each breath of air wafted down on the fresh green sward beneath, the snowy petals, where they nestled amid the golden heads of the dandelions, like pearls in a setting of emerald and gold.

The girl's look wandered far off over the radiant landscape, and her hands fell idly in her lap as she gazed. In tender brown, fast taking on their destined verdure, or in delicate green that blended richly with the deeper hues of the fir and hemlock, the forests stretched out their aisles of beauty. While far away in the west a line of hills lifted peaks only less blue than the sky that bent above them. Beneath such a sky, so blue, flecked with clouds of such fleecy whiteness as no painter's skill can ever produce, and over all the waves of golden sunlight like the smile of God, what wonder that she gazed in rapture and adoring gratitude?'

Far away down the white road, she could see the figure of a man coming slowly and wearily on, with bent form and bowed head, and the girl thought how desolate he looked amid all the surrounding brightness.

Then resuming her sewing, she forgot the wayfarer, till a sudden shadow fell across her work, causing her to glance upward. The man she had seen stood just by the window under the shade of the apple trees.

Mary started at the suddenness of his appearance, and the worn, haggard look of the face turned so eagerly toward her, as though its owner would read her soul.

"Are you Mary Bradley/" he asked, lifting his hat, and revealing a tangled mass of iron gray hair that fell low over his weather beaten forehead.

"Yes, sir, did you wish to see me?" Mary answered her voice always low and sweet, now sweeter than ever for the pity, which the man's appearance excited.

"I'm Jim Staples, Old Jim Staples, who used to live down at the corner, and I've come a long way to tell you that your prayer is answered. I'm trying to do better, and so I hope I shall meet my wife."

Mary Bradley started up with a quick cry. Throwing open the door, she held out her hand with the welcoming words, "You don't know, Mr. Staples, how glad I am to hear you say that. Come right in, and then I want to know all about how you have learned to love God and all you please to tell me of yourself. You could not have brought me more welcome news."

The man came gladly in, with the happiest look that Mary ever remembered to have seen there, playing over his features. Laying down his hat and staff, he took the chair she placed for him. Then he said, abruptly, "You prayed for me, didn't you?"

"Yes, sir, and somehow I've always believed I should know that my prayers were answered sometime before I died."

"You said, that last day I came here, that you'd always remember to pray for me, and that other little gal that was here sick, Holton's gal, warn't it? She said, you know, that your prayers were all answered. I kept a thinking and a thinking of your promise, and what she said about it, and how kind you both spoke to me. Do what I would; I couldn't get rid of the thinking.

"I went down East a logging, and got among a rougher set of men than I, bad as I am, ever got amongst before. Nights where they were drinking, and gambling, and swearing, and singing their vile songs, I'd happen to think of what you said, and many a time I've gone off by myself to think. I couldn't bear that my remembrances of you should come 'mongst all that smoke and noise. By and by they noticed it, and used to laugh at me, and then I'd get mad, and swear back at them, till they were glad enough to let me alone.

"I guess I was as bad any of them before the first year was out. The worse I grew, the more I hated myself, and the worse it made me feel to think anybody as good as you are, was praying for such a miserable wretch as I was. Then I'd drink to forget all about it, and as like as not, get into a terrible quarrel, and all the while, you were praying, warn't you?"

"I never forgot you," Mary answered, and then the man went on again with his story,

"I kept going on, worse and worse, and twice I got shut up in jail for some of my wicked doings. Till I got so I didn't much care what did become of me. Till nigh on to a year ago, I'd quarreled worse than ever with the men I was working with. The whole gang were ag'in me, and I picked up my traps and started on for a new place.

It was an awful hot day. I went on and on, and partly from the heat and partly from the whiskey I had drunk the night before, I didn't get over many miles when night came on, and there I was, in the darkest piece of woods I ever saw. You see, I'd tried to take a beeline for the next logging camp down the river, and rather missed in my reckoning, and there I was. I swore horridly, and drank what I had left in my whiskey bottle. It seemed to grow dark amazin' quick, and the trees were so thick I couldn't tell what the matter was, till, all at once, the rain came down on the trees above me, and then such lightening and thunder came as I never saw or heard afore. I used to boast that I warn't afraid o' nothing, but I was scart then, and I did what I hadn't done for years before, I got down on my knees and prayed.

" 'Twarn't much of a prayer, I only said, 'O Lord don't kill me, I aint fit to die, don't kill me, and I'll live a different life, if I can only find out how to do it,' and I kept saying this over and over ag'in. There was the wind a blowing, and the rain coming down in buckets full, and the lighting flashing all the time and such a roaring of thunder! Every now and then I could hear the trees come crashing down, and the screams of some of the wild varmints that live about there. There I was a praying and a praying, and scart as any woman. It lasted way into the night, and there I lay on the wet ground, soberer than I'd been afore in months. I broke my whiskey bottle, and I'm afraid I swore, I'd got so used to it, that I never would drink another drop as long as I lived."

"Haven't you drank any since? Mary asked while old Mrs. Hammond, who had come into the room, sat looking at the strange visitor in much wonder.

"No, Miss, not a drop. I've been tempted more times than I can number, but I've somehow been kept from it. Well, I stayed there all night, and I guess all the bad I ever did came into my mind. I thought how I'd treated my poor wife, and what a good angel you was to her, and how happy she died, and everything seemed worse than I ever saw it before, and I rolled on the ground in my agony.

"After a long while it began to grow light, and I got up and went on. I was weak and faint, and it took me till long past noon to get to the camp I was bound for, and then I was so beat out that I didn't do a stroke o' work for more'n a week. There were several downright good Christian men in that camp, and when they talked to me, I didn't swear at them and threaten them, as I'd been used to doing. But I told them just what an old wretch I was, and how I'd promised to be better, if God would spare me, that night o' the thundershower. Miss, they kept at work, preaching and praying, and schooling me in the right way, till somehow, after a while, I lost my burden. Like as poor Pilgrim did his, that it tells about in a book one of them used to read aloud evenings, and I felt just as ready to serve God then as I'd been to serve the devil before."

"You learned to love the dear Saviour, and trust in Him?"

"Love Him! I can't tell you how much I love Him. He's done so much for me, why I was wickeder than the thief on the cross, and yet He died for me, and such as me. The lumbermen are a rough set, rougher than you can think anything about, but when they learn to love God, they don't make any halfway work about it. Some of the men called our camp a 'Bethel in the wilderness,' and we did have blessed times there, I assure you. I didn't have to go off by myself when I wanted to think about you and how you were praying.

"There were some things I wanted to do, and so three months ago I went back to the old camp. The men looked kind o' wonder struck to see me, but I told them the straightforward truth. Though some of 'em swore, and some of 'em laughed, I didn't flinch. God helped my poor old tongue to talk to 'em. His gospel was so much the strongest, that half a dozen of the very worst, Bill Sykes among 'em, couldn't stand out ag'st it, and they were all converted in less than a fortnight.

There was one droll fellow, kind hearted when he hadn't any whiskey aboard, but the hardest fellow to swear and fight when a little riled with drinking. So funny in his oaths that the rest used to try to get him mad, just for the fun of hearing him get up the strangest ways of swearing anybody ever heard of. I don't know as you'll believe this, but 'tis certain true, for I heard him myself. He used to be always singing songs. A day or two after he was converted, we heard him singing at a great rate. Another man and I went to see what the trouble could be, it sounded so droll. I thought he must be crazy at first, for there he was, thrashing about him with a great stick, and shouting away. Now this is as true as the gospel, Miss, he was shouting and singing, 'Chase the devil round a stump, and hit him a rap at every jump.'

"I should have thought him crazy, I'm sure," Mary exclaimed, with a laugh. "What did you say to him?"

"I listened a spell and then I asked, for he was so taken up with his thrashing and singing, that he didn't see us, 'What's going on, Tom? What kind of a tantrum do you call this?'"

"'Why,' said he, 'I'm so chock full of happiness, I must do something! So I'm letting off steam in this way.' And Miss, he was just as sincere in his rejoicing and loving God as any of the folks that go to church all dressed up in their best clothes, and sing hymns, set to proper tunes, in a proper manner. When I came off, he told me that he was bound to fight the devil, and if God only helped him, he guessed he should conquer him. I tell you, there's lots of serving God in the world that would look and sound droll enough to folks that never roughed it as I have."

"Yes," said old Mrs. Hammond, "It takes all sorts of folks to make the world, and some, when they're brought to God, show their religion one way, and some another, but it'll shine out some way, if they've only got it."

"That's my doctrine," the man answered, then stopping for his hat, he continued, "I've done two of the things I wanted to. I've told them at the old camp how I've learned to love Jesus, and I've let you know that your prayers are answered, that you've prayed me right, after this long while, and how there's one thing more, yes, two things, and then I'm going back to logging ag'in. I should have been here sooner, but I had a sick spell, apiece back, and that belated me a good three weeks, and I hain't got my strength up yet. I want to get a little stone to mark my wife's grave. I would like, if they'll only let me, to tell how the Lord has converted me, so that all the good people here, who knew how bad I was, may get strength and faith to keep on praying for sinners. Do you think they'll let such a rough old fellow as I speak in a meetin'?"

"Indeed, they will rejoice to hear you, and I can't tell how happy what you have said has made me," said Mary.

"God only knows how much I thank you, dear miss Mary, for the good your life and your talk and your praying has done me. Then you were so kind to my poor wife; she used to say that she wished you were her gal. I've felt these long years that if I could give you something that you could wear, and remember me by, I should like to ever so much. Lately I've wanted more than ever before to bring you something, and last week I got this, and now if you won't be ashamed to take a gift from such an old sinner as I have been, I shall feel wonderfully pleased. He placed in Mary's hand a beautiful white knitted shawl, with delicate light pink flowers and outlined with elegant lace.

Mary burst into tears, the very humility with which the gift was offered was touching in the extreme. As soon as she could command her voice, she said, holding out her hand to grasp that of the old man,

"Accept it? Indeed I will sir, though I have done nothing for you to merit such a gift. I derived as much pleasure, I think, as your wife did from what I did for her, and in praying for you, I only followed the Bible command, 'always to pray and not to faint.''

"But such a wretched old sinner as I was! I heard of somebody's saying that 'twould do no good to pray for me. I was too far gone for prayers to do me any good, and I know I was awful wicked, you don't know how wicked."

"All the more need of prayers, then," said Mary. "I don't believe in anybody's being too wicked to pray for. Oh, sir, don't go, please stay and have tea with us, and indeed we can make you comfortable for the night, and as long as you choose to stay with us."

The man hesitated, and Mrs. Hammond added to Mary's reiterated invitation, "Do stay, by all means, sir, you look weak and tired, and 'twould be a shame for us to let you go further tonight. Besides, you're a brother in Christ, and to such, more than to all others, we are commanded to do good."

"But I'm dusty and worn with walking, and I don't want to make trouble."

"You won't make a bit of trouble, and if you'll only let me, I'll be glad to repair your clothes, and you can wear some of Father's while I'm doing it," Mary urged, earnestly.

"You'll be sure to get the blessing," he replied, reseating himself, and once more laying down his hat.

"What blessing, sir? I'm only doing what is both duty and pleasure."

"A pleasure to have me here?"

"Yes, sir, a real pleasure, and I shall gladden my next letter to Father by telling him all about it."

"Well, I meant the blessing that will be pronounced when the judgment day comes, on those who have shown kindness to one of the least of the followers of Christ, you know they'll inherit a kingdom. Now you speak of telling your father, just as though I was worth his caring anything about.

Why, the very last time I saw your father, Miss Mary, I talked shamefully to him, and he didn't answer back again, as I hoped he would, but showed by his actions and words that he'd got something in his heart that I hadn't got. I tried that several times, and I found he wouldn't let his temper get the better of him. Can you know this, and still want me to stay, and think that your father will want to know anything about me?"

"That's all past and gone. I really don't believe Father has ever given those things you speak of a second thought, and if he has, he's forgiven you long ago, I'm sure, and he'd want you to stay if he were only here."

"I thought I should creep into one of those empty cabins down by the railroad, and stay tonight. I didn't suppose anybody here would let me stay in their barns even. I heard one man say as I came through the village, today, 'There's that drunken old vagabond, Staples, back here ag'in. I thought the world was rid of him long ago.' I stopped and asked somebody if you was alive yet and your father. The men I asked seemed to think it a fine thing to bother an old man, for he asked me if I thought a young lady like Mary Bradley would notice such an old cuss as I was? I told him if you was as good as you used to be you would, and he laughed and said, 'Go ahead, old fellow.'"

"I'm sorry any one should be so disrespectful, and I am glad to see you. I'm glad you should believe it, and feel at home here long as you stay." Mary sweetly told him.

"You're not one bit ashamed to have me here?"

"Ashamed! No, indeed, and now, as Mrs. Hammond has tea all ready, we will go and enjoy that."

"You'll have to excuse my roughness. I never had much manners taught me when I was young, and I hain't been where I should make what I did have any better, for the last eight years, and over."

"We'll excuse everything," said Mary, and led the way to the tea table.

"I'm wonderfully chocked up," the poor man said. Later in the evening he took his lamp to retire. "'You're a blessed set, all of you, and I'm glad I came home. It does me a power of good to have you like that shawl. I was afraid you'd say you wouldn't take it, and I'd got my mind on your having it."

"I thank you, sir, many, many times," and Mary's face glowed with the earnestness of her feelings.

The next morning Mr. Staples was too ill to rise, and he continued so for several days, indeed the doctor feared he might never recover. He had evidently over tasked his strength in his efforts to reach Martinsville so soon after a severe sickness. But at last, a naturally good constitution triumphed, with the aid of God's blessing on faithful nursing, and glad indeed were the whole family when the sufferer was convalescent. His patient endurance of his often acute pain, and his humble Christian demeanor were fast endearing him to all their hearts, while Dr. Osborne was also much interested in the quaint ideas that found utterance in still quainter words.

It was far into June before he was able to attend church, and the quiet, humble looking, gray haired man who followed Mary into the pew, looked little like the insolent drunkard of years gone by. As he so much desired, he told his story in the prayer meeting. Among the unusual attendants who came out of curiosity to hear, as was said by more than one, "what that miserable old wanderer had to say for himself," were several of his boon companions in younger days, one of whom was pricked to the heart, and soon after was rejoicing to share his old friend's hope.

He procured a suitable stone to mark his wife's resting place, and planted some evergreens around. While Mary promised, if she lived, to plant flowers about the lowly bed when the spring should come again. He procured light work in the neighborhood till his strength was sufficiently recovered for his return to Maine, where he felt that he might be able to labor among the lumbermen, as one less acquainted with them would be unable to do.

"Most likely you won't see me again, Mary," he said at starting, "I'm growing old faster than I should if I had served God instead of the Evil One, when I was young. Satan is a bad taskmaster, and pays in poor coin, besides. I don't expect to live many years, but I hope you may, and that your life may be full of blessings here, as I know 'twill be in heaven.

I'll meet you up there, and 'twon't be such a long time before we shall have to go, even if we live to grow as old as anybody ever lives to be now a days," and, wiping the tears from his furrowed checks, he pressed Mary's hand fondly and departed.

His presence had been a great comfort to the girl, and she missed his cheering words, even though they were often rough and uncouth when the news of some terrible battle came. She waited anxiously for tidings of her father's safety. He had been slightly wounded twice, and Mary, though trustful of God's care, could not but feel a great weight of dread and uncertainty in regard to his fate.

She maintained a regular and pleasant correspondence with Lucy Day, and through her, often received cheering messages from Susan, who, in the midst of her pain and weakness, was still giving her earnest efforts to bless the soldiers and all connected with them.

It had been a pleasant surprise when, in the gentle sufferer of whose labors Bro. Rand had so touchingly spoken; she had recognized the precious sister of whom Lucy often wrote. Late in October, by her father's express request, she accepted an oft-repeated invitation to visit her former teacher, and found a hearty welcome among the Days.

Fred was out as chaplain in the army, and his wife and child were at the homestead. While John, who, for his father's sake, long delayed going, but at length was sent away with a blessing. He had been rapidly climbing the ladder of honor, till his sisters laughingly paraded, in their letters to him, their fear of the brave Gen. Day, of whom so many noble things were told, but who to them was still simply "Brother John.' Dearer to them by this sweet home title than by any won on the battlefield, however they might rejoice in his well earned fame.

Willie was still in college, while Anna was wearing the crown of patience, for the months that had passed might be multiplied by many before she could hope to say welcoming words to the one with whom she hoped to share life's joys and trials.

"The bell tolled this morning for a funeral," remarked Mr. Day as he came in at diner hour one day soon after Mary Bradley's arrival.

"I wonder who can be dead," someone else said While from another came, " 'Tis some old person. I counted when they struck the age and made out sixty-four strokes. I can't think who it can be. Had you heard that any one was ill, Father?"

"I know who it is," said one of the farm hands who had been to the village and just then came in, 'tis old Howard, the walk about. They found him dead in the woods, yesterday morning, and he's to be buried at two o'clock this afternoon."

"Poor old friend! He has died as the fool dieth," said Mr. Day, sadly. "I have often feared some such ending to his godless, reckless life. Neither wife nor child to watch over his last moments, or follow him to his grave."

"Let us go to the funeral, Father" suggested Lucy, "and perhaps Mary will like to go with us." So, an hour later, Mr. Day with the two girls rode over to the church where the services were to be performed.

Little like the rich trappings that marked his daughter's last obsequies, or the scarcely less rich surroundings of his wife'' funeral, was the plain coffin of stained pine, destitute alike of ornament and varnish.

Not a relative in the seats usually occupied by the mourners, for Mr. Howard in early youth had come from a distance to win riches and a home among strangers, and none of his friends were near enough to be summoned to his funeral. There were a few friends of his wife in a neighboring town, but there had been but little intercourse between them and him for a long time, and they chose to remain away.

It was little that the minister who led the services could say in commendation of the departed, and after briefly alluding to his long and eventful life among them, and to his sad lonely death, bereft of the comforts of home and the watchful care of affection, he continued,

"We cannot tell, God only can know, what his last thoughts were, and how his last moments were occupied. It may possibly be that, even at the eleventh hour, and with his wasted mental powers, he went at last to the fountain of all consolation, repeating the publican's prayer, 'God be merciful to me a sinner.' We have no means of judging, and so must leave him, and the solemn issues that wait upon death, to the merciful and all wise Ruler of the universe.

"But to us comes this lesson, this most solemn of all lessons, that a life of godliness, a life wrought into peace and harmony with God's will, a life consecrated to and filled with Christ, can alone give the assurance of happy death and a blissful eternity. There are deathbed repentances, but if we neglect God while in health, we do not know that sickness will give us reason or strength for matters of such vital importance. Nor are we sure of even that warning that our days are numbered, that comes with sickness, we may be stricken down at any moment, without an instant's notice, and then where is the room for repentance? 'Too late! Too late!' will be the requiem wailed by many despairing souls. Too late for repentance, too late for the joys of pardoned sin, too late for rendering service to Him who went about doing good, too late to win others to Christ, too late to pray, too late to praise, too late for everything but the ceaseless agony of remorse, and the longing for the bliss never to be realized. Can you look on that dead face and not receive this lesson into your hearts? A godless life, except in rare instances, ends in a godless death.

It was a sad funeral, sadder even than when friends gather around the open grave, where oftentimes it seems as though their very hearts were buried with the departed, and from more than one heart the cry went up, "Lord, save me from such a fate."

"I wonder if Harry Howard has ever been heard from?" Lucy questioned on their way home.

"I heard some one say this afternoon," said her father, "that rumors have reached town that he is in the rebel army. He has been recognized by some of our men, when, in doing picket duty, the guards on the opposite sides have come quite near each other."

"What a kind hearted, merry boy he was! I can scarcely believe that all this change has been wrought in both our family and that of the Howards since those happy days when Laura and I went to school together, and Harry was our most devoted champion at all the merry makings of the neighborhood. I hardly seemed to know the difference between him and my own brothers, and now only Harry is left of that whole family, and amid what sins, temptations and perils he is living is unknown to us all."

A surprise awaited them on their arrival home, and by no means an unpleasant one. In Susan's bright room they found Justin Rand who had come, so he told them, "to get a little sunshine." He had seen Mr. Bradley but a short time previous to his starting for home, and both Fred and John within a few weeks. In his encouraging account of the absent, he brought, so Lucy told him, sunshine with him.

From Fred he was the bearer of a package of letters. Lucy's letter brought with it the oft desired solution of the question, "Where is Harry Howard?"

Fred wrote, "A week ago, a squad of our men brought in half a dozen prisoners, all more or less seriously wounded. In the person of one of them I soon recognized Harry Howard, though it wouldn't have been strange had I failed to do so. Haggard and dirty in the extreme, one arm shattered at the elbow, and his clothes in tatters and bespattered with blood, I don't believe you would have know him.

"These men were taken to the hospital, as they were all suffering from their undressed wounds, and the assistant surgeon being away, I went to aid Dr. Brown as I might be needed. When Harry saw me, he turned his head away with a deep groan and the most agonized look I ever saw on a man' face, full of anguish as I have seen many since I have been here. I was shocked, and then in an instant came the thought; perhaps he's been brought here to find the 'open door.'

"I laid my hand on his, and said as calmly as I could, 'I'm sorry to see an old friend in so sad a condition, Harry.'

"He turned fiercely toward me, and with an oath said, 'Amazingly sorry I fancy you are, Day. You'll have a fine chance to fill your pocket by giving me up to the government. There have been great rewards offered for my detection and capture. Now's your time, but I tell you, man, that you'll have to work spry. I shall kick the bucket and go to the bottom soon, I reckon.'

" 'Don't talk so, Harry,' I answered, 'I haven't a thought of doing anything to injure you in any way, and I am not desirous to load my purse by such means. I want to do you good.'

"'A sight of good you'll do me, I reckon, so you needn't preach any to me. I've lived thus far without troubling myself about such things, and I shan't begin now.'

"So much venom did he put into these words that I could not refrain from saying, 'And a wretched piece of work you've made of living, I should think you would desire to find something better.'

"He only answered with an oath, and bade that surgeon, who was ready to attend him, be quick with his work. An hour afterwards, when we had dressed his wounds, thoroughly bathed him, and given him the luxury of clean clothes and a bed in the hospital, as I held a soothing draught to his lips, he looked up with a gentler expression, and said, respectfully and gratefully, 'Fred, don't lay up what I have said, I'm sorry you always was a good fellow. I believe you mean to do right, whatever happens.'

"He's been failing ever since, and though often terribly profane, he yet, now and then, listens patiently. Today he turned suddenly round and said, 'There's only one person in the world who can lead me to like religion, and that person is your sister Lucy. I believe in her, as I don't in anything or anybody else. I know I'm going to die, and I'd give the world to see her once more. I'm a wretched, miserable fellow, and I shouldn't blame her if she felt ashamed to be seen speaking to me, but I should run the risk if I could only go home. She's an angel, if ever there was one on earth, and if my mother and Laura had been more like her, I might have been a different man.'

"I did not dare to encourage him, but, Lucy, I want you, if possible, to come back with Justin. I feel that the salvation of this wretched man lies largely in your hands. God seems to have given it to you, and the time in which you can work will be brief. His wounds are not particularly dangerous, but the surgeon says he is dying of disease. Duty has been your mistress heretofore, don't fail to honor her now."

"Go, by all means," was the unanimous decision of the whole family, when Lucy laid Harry's case and Fred's request before them.

A week later, a quiet little brown robed figure stepped from an ambulance at the entrance of a well known hospital, taken possession of by Chaplain Day, and led away to the nurses' quarters. Leaving her there, Fred went to the ward where Harry was lying and sitting beside him, asked if he was certain his desire could be granted, what his most earnest wish would be.

A look of wistful agony flitted over his pale face, as in feeble accents he answered, "I suppose I ought to say that I should like to be ready to die, but I shan't. I tell you, Fred, I'd rather see your sister Lucy than enjoy any happiness I can possibly imagine."

"What if I should tell you that my sister is here, and has come on purpose to see you and help you?"

Harry started up with a low cry, and then, sinking on his pillow again, said piteously, "You can't be cruel enough to deceive me, but this seems too good to be true."

Just then Fred saw the brown dress, and the fair face, lighted with tender compassion, gleaming about it, and beckoning her forward, this gentle sister of his, so pure in her womanly grace, he placed her in his seat by the sick man's couch and moved away. The hot tears rushed from their hidden fountains to Lucy's eyes, as she took the emaciated hand of the sufferer and uttered her kindly greeting. Harry was too deeply moved for words, and tried in vain to answer, while she smoothed away the tangle of brown curls, in which, young as he was, threads of silver were here and there visible, from his hot brow, and went on talking in her quiet, sisterly way. She had gone to him, determined to let no prejudice or any kindred feeling deter her from the fullest discharge of the duties she desired to assume as nurse and teacher, and thus, God willing, save a soul.

The sick man had been sleeplessly wretched during the previous night, now the soothing touch of her hand quieted him, and the heavy lids fell over the sunken but brilliant eyes. Two or three times she thought he was asleep, and then with a start he would open his eyes and look wildly around, and on meeting her reassuring smile, would sink to sleep again.

Once he whispered, "I was afraid I was dreaming, and should wake up and find you were not here."

"But you see I am here, and you may sleep undisturbed. I think you will find me here when you awake," Lucy answered. As if obedient to her wishes, he sank into the most refreshing slumber that he had enjoyed for days. Lucy maintained her position by his side, and during the two hours that he slept, her heart was sending its voiceless petitions to the throne of infinite mercy.

When at last the heavy lids opened, she was startled at the abruptness of Harry's first words.

"I am afraid I shan't prove a very apt scholar, Miss Lucy, I have been so thoughtless and full of sin all my life, but I'll try hard. I have got to die, and I should like to know how my sins might be forgiven, and I may find a Christian's peace. God knows I'm wretched enough over my sins, and I would try and repair some of the evil I have done, if my life could only be spared. That I can't hope for, but I would like to learn how I may be saved."

Harry had uttered these words painfully, and with intervals of coughing between, and when he stopped through weakness, Lucy said, "'Believe on the Lord Jesus Christ, and thou shalt be saved.'"

"Teach me how to believe," he said, simply.

With eternity staring him in the face, the self-confidence and skeptical foolhardiness of his earlier days faded into a worthless dream. Many times during the days that followed did the thought, "Like a little child," flit through Lucy's mind. She repeated, again and again, the story of the cross, and the willingness of Christ to save the vilest, and marked the humble earnestness with which he received her plainest spoken words, that would once, had she applied them to him, have aroused his bitterest contempt and anger.

She devoted a large share of her time to his comfort, reading, singing and conversing. Some of the poor fellows, lying near, listened eagerly to her words, and one fair haired youth, some mother's pet and darling, waiting patiently for the healing of severe wounds, told Fred in confidence, that the crumbs of truth which fell to his share were a feast of themselves.

Morning, noon and night, when her light step paused beside the pallet of some sufferer, for a moment's talk, a kind inquiry, a comforting word, or a bit of pleasant news, heavy eyes would brighten. At last, someone having a vein of poetry about him named her "The Star of the Hospital." The regiment to which Fred was attached was on guard, and stationed in the vicinity of the hospital, and he, having considerable leisure, devoted much time to the sick and wounded therein.

As a child clings confidingly to its mother's guiding hand, so Harry Howard, as his strength ebbed away, clung the closer to Lucy's teachings. Till, gathering power and confidence, prayed for forgiveness and mercy as light dawned slowly on his mind, his hope of pardon and peace, at first weak and uncertain, grew into that good hope that maketh not ashamed, but laid hold upon that within the veil.

"I shall get to heaven," he said one day, when after a careful examination, the surgeon had told him that his remnant of life was probably limited to a few days. "I believe I shall get safely there, but I shall have a starless crown. I shan't be able to do anything to show my love for the Saviour who has pardoned me, nothing whatever, I can only give Him this poor, worn out, earth saddened heart, with all its corruption, its scars of pride, anger and filth. It seems to me that, if I could live, the longest life ever allotted man would be too short to show the love and thankfulness I feel toward the Lord Jesus, but his is not for me. I can't show the world how I love Him, nor counteract the evil I have done by a better life and a more holy conversation."

"You can honor Him by suffering patiently," Lucy said encouragingly, "perhaps that is the way He has appointed for you to serve Him. Taking His pardon as a free gift, you mustn't keep looking back to the slough of despond and ways of iniquity where your feet have wandered so long, but look ahead, to the rest that remaineth for you, for me, for us all, if we seek it truly. Someone has called heaven a 'hill country,' and the idea is beautiful, for to reach it implies the need of a constant looking up. The more we 'look up' the more light we get, and the less we see of the weariness and griefs and temptations that lie all along the way."

"Won't you read that, Miss Day?" and the occupant of the next pallet reached toward her a small book on the flyleaf of which was written, "The Lord knoweth how to deliver the godly out of temptation." 2 Peter 2:9 The words were these,

> "The while in peace abiding,
> Within a sheltered home,
> We feel that sin and sorrow
> Can never never come,
> But let the strong temptations sweep,
> As whirlwinds sweep the sea,
> We find no strength to 'scape the wreck,
> Save, pitying God, in thee."

"That is indeed beautiful," Lucy said, "and no less true than beautiful. I learned a few verses the other day that I think you may like, Harry, and perhaps our friend here will like them also."

Then while all within reach of her voice were hushed into almost breathless quiet in their eagerness to hear, she repeated, with a sweet distinctness that carried the pleasure of listening to quite a distance up and down the ward, Whittier's "Wish of Today." The lines are worth reproducing,

> "I ask not now for gold to gild
> With mocking shine a weary frame,
> The yearning of the mind is stilled
> I ask not now for Fame.
>
> A rose cloud dimly seen above,
> Melting in heaven's blue depths away
> O! sweet, fond dream of human Love,
> For thee I may not pray.

> But, bowed in lowliness of mind,
> I make my humble wishes known
> I only ask a will resigned,
> O, father, to thine own!
>
> Today, beneath thy chastening eye,
> I crave alone for peace and rest,
> Submissive in thy hand to lie,
> And feel that it is best.
>
> And now my spirit sighs for home,
> And longs for light whereby to see,
> And like a weary child, would come,
> O Father, unto thee!

The stillness that enfolds and follows rapt attention gave Lucy the assurance that the great beauty of the poem was fully appreciated, and after a little time, she said, taking Harry's thin hand in hers,

"Is this your prayer, also? Do you wish to find peace and rest, and lie submissive in His upholding hand?"

"The lines shape my unspoken wishes into words in a wonderful manner, but" he added, while his lips curved into a smile of thankfulness, and his eyes glistened with tears, "I would like to have a stanza or two in addition, rounded into the perfect fullness of praise that I should like to render God for his great goodness to me, so unworthy as I am."

The conversation turned upon Laura, Harry's sister.

"The last few years of her life," said Lucy, "I utterly neglected any personal effort. To be sure I never forgot to pray for her, but I allowed a sinful fear to prevent my urging, by either going to see her myself or by writing to her, the great claims of religion upon her."

"She slighted all your earlier efforts, did she not?" Harry asked.

"Yes, but I ought not to have been discouraged at that, you know we should labor in season and out of season. I failed in this."

"Not failed, you should not say that, you say you never forgot to pray for her, and you read to me only yesterday that 'prayer is the strongest weapon that can be brought to bear against the hosts of sin.' I don't think the sin of neglect lies at your dóor, she had shunned you for years, and you had no opportunity to see her, and I do not believe appeals either by written or spoken words would have won you aught but insult."

"But that ought not to have hindered me, God might have softened her heart to listen."

"We must leave it all with God. Please sing 'Rock of Ages; before you leave, he pleaded, as Lucy rose to go away. Reseating herself, she complied.

" 'Rock of Ages, cleft for me,' " repeated Harry. The tones of her voice died away and then the sufferer slept.

That night Harry Howard died. Just at midnight a messenger came for Lucy, with the tiding that he was sinking. Hastening to his side, she found Fred already with him, while the dying man's breath came wearily through his pallid lips. As Lucy bent over him, he tried to raise his hand to clasp hers, while she understanding the movement, took in her warm grasp the icy fingers, and wiped tenderly the death damp from his temples. In a few earnest words, Fred commended the spirit of their dying friend to the merciful care of God, and then, only as they now and then spoke holy words of cheer and promise, they watched in silence while the wave of life ebbed and flowed, in the last struggle.

Pale, frightened faces looked up from the couches, up and down the long ward. Death was no unusual visitor among them, but the frequency of this return had not robbed him of his terrors, and who could tell to which one of them his next summons might be addressed? Silently as possible the night nurses moved among them, and the wary surgeon went his rounds, for the hospital was crowded, and his duties were very arduous.

When the first golden gleam of morning appeared in the east, the sufferer, who had seem hardly conscious for the last hour, opened his eyes and fixed his gaze on Lucy, his lips moved and she bent to listen.

"Going soon," he said faintly, "and I die blessing you, thanking God for you."

"Are you happy?" asked Fred.

"Happier than ever before in life."

"And Jesus is precious, and blesses you with His presence?"

"He is my all, and I can trust Him, He is with me."

He spoke with difficulty, and soon sank into a fitful slumber. Once they thought he had ceased to breathe, but he looked up once more, with a beautiful smile lighting up his countenance, and with the words, spoken with more strength than for some time previous, "My Saviour calls me," gasped a few times and was gone.

Tears fell fast, but they were not hopeless tears. His death had been too full of peace, too blessed with the divine presence, to allow that. Indeed there was more of joy than grief in their flow, when they remembered the great change that the last few weeks had wrought in him, and the still greater change that had, "Burst his prison bars, one moment here so low, and now beyond the stars."

Rest was written all over the quiet face, and was eloquent in the peaceful smile that rested thereon.

To many he was only the 'rebel soldier,' and with simply, "Poor fellow! He's got his discharge, he can't fight against Justice and right anymore," and other similar expressions. He passed away from their remembrance, but to Fred and Lucy it was as though some sweet assurance had been given them that their friend was theirs for all eternity, "not lost, but gone before."

They buried him under a clump of pines in one corner of the little burying place attached to the hospital grounds, and felt, as they stood beside his grave, that the last few weeks, with the closing scene, had been the best part of his life.

In a few days Lucy returned north, and in the quiet joys of home found the rest she was needing.

Chapter XIV
Conclusion

After war comes peace, after storm, sunshine, after sorrow, joy's completest fruition, and so to our stricken and strife torn land came the "Peace Autumn."

Mary Bradley's father came out of the struggle safely, and so, too, did John and Fred Day, and as in these, so in multitudes of other homes, Te Deaums was sung from the depths of rejoicing hearts.

Stephen Bradley came back to his pleasant home with the expectation of spending his days there, but providence had arranged it differently, and with the next summer's roses God gave Mary a broader sphere of usefulness as the wife of John Day. She had been faithful in a little, and so more was given her.

Her father could not endure the thought of being separated from her, and so followed her to her new abode to share its joys with her.

Anna had passed under the rod of affliction far away from home. Her betrothed had met his sad, lingering death at Belle Isle, and only after long, dreary months of anxious and uncertain waiting, did she even have the sad comfort of knowing that he had passed beyond the reach of cruelty and suffering. It was a heavy blow, and only that Christ was her burden bearer, she would have sunk beneath it. She learned to say from the depths of a heart full of confidence in God's love and wisdom, "He doeth all things well" "the Lord gave, and the Lord hath taken away, blessed be the name of the Lord.

Conclusion

Justin Rand was an honored and beloved pastor, and when he asked Lucy to share his labors, she had accepted her life mission, and gone humbly to new duties.

Just before Mary Bradley left Martinsville, Grandma Brewer went to her grave in the full fruition of a ripe old age, and, only a few days later, Alice Osborne's young life, sorrowful, yet full of hope, triumphing even in death, ended here, to find a brighter sphere in Heaven. She had been failing slowly for months, but on that day had seemed unusually strong and cheerful. Just at sunset she complained of being very weary and saying to her mother, "I'm so tired, I'm going to say, 'Now I lay me down to sleep,' just as I used to when I was a little girl, and then go to sleep, she nestled her head down and went quietly to rest. When her brother came in to bid her "Good night," she had gone where there is no night. She had said her prayer and gone to sleep, the sleep that God giveth His beloved.

Blanche, with her husband and little ones, was leading her happy useful life, the days rounding into completeness amid duties faithfully performed and blessing thankfully received. While in her the poor, the sorrowful, the unfortunate and sin laden always found a helping hand, and heart full of all tender compassion and earnest counsels to seek the sure "Ark of Refuge."

The blessed truths of revealed religion had proved to her "the shadow of a great rock in a weary land," and she longed to see all around her yielding to its influence. Her father she had never heard from, both her older sisters had died, while the younger members of the family were following in her steps and "clinging to the cross,' which had long been both her support and comfort.

"Here's a droll looking letter from 'way down east,' Mary," John Day announced as he came home one night, at the same time tossing into her lap an uncouth looking epistle, which having been sent to "Miss Mary Bradley," at Martinsville, had been re-directed and forwarded to her present home.

"It must be from Mr. Staples," answered Mary, at the same time removing the envelope. But no, it was signed, "Martin Hines," and read as follows,

"Dear Miss, I take my pen in hand to let you know that poor old Staples is dead. He made me promise that I would do my best to write to you, and let you know all about him. He hain't been well for a long spell, and used to talk a heap about you, and how much good you had done him, and how he hoped to see you in Heaven.

Jim Staples was good, and he's been the means of bringing dozens of us to see how full of sin we were, and how God was waiting to pardon us, if we only went to Him. Then he'd tell us his story, and how you prayed him out of the sinful ways he had walked in so long, and what a blessing you was to everybody. He had a package done up the day before he died, and left it in my care, for he knew, rough as I am, he could trust me, and wanted, when I found to whether you was living or not, that I should send it to you. I've got it safe, and just as soon as you get this, I wish you would let me know, for I wouldn't miss of your having the bundle, for he set his heart on it so. He said you always prayed for him, and now that he won't need being prayed for any longer, I hope you'll still remember that there's hundreds of others, just such lonely old fellows as he was that need praying for.

I hope you'll overlook all my blunders and poor writing, for I ain't much of a scholar, and don't write a letter once in a dog's age."

With a repetition of the request that she would write very soon, and giving the address to which her letter must be sent, the epistle ended.

"Poor old man!" mused Mary, as she refolded her letter.

"Rather say, rich blessed old man," replied her husband, who, leaning on their chair had shared her perusal of its contents.

"Rich and beyond compare happy, I have no doubt," she returned. "Still I could never think of his lonely life for the past few years, since he learned life's worth and purpose without feeling a pitiful desire that he might have enjoyed more fully the privileges of worshipping God among those who would have encouraged and helped him."

'I should judge from this letter that he had been faithful to the souls around him, and God gives all needed strength and blessing to his faithful followers. From what you have before told me of him, I rather think he was well fitted for missionary labor among the rough men with whom his lot was cast. He was one with them, and could understand their needs as you or I would have failed to do."

"That was what he used to say, when people urged him to remain at Martinsville. He thought he could do more for God there with the rough backwoodsmen than he could find to do where people were better educated, and knew so much more than he did."

"God fits us all for out station if we only look for guiding circumstances, and oftentimes I believe lets us pass through some experience, painful it may be in the extreme, that we may better understand how to hold the cup of consolation to other sorrowful lips. There's a purpose in everything, and what sister Mary so often says about 'all evil being good a making,' is rich with a vein of truth. Evil is always evil of itself, but in God's hands it may be overruled so as to bring to pass a vast good to some one. So I presume the peculiar circumstances of Mr. Staples' life gave him a clearer insight into his companions' character than any amount of education cold have done."

In due time, after Mary's reply to her letter, the package reached her. It contained the savings of the last few years of his life, and a rudely penned note, begging her to accept the whole from one who felt that he owed all the real happiness of this life, and the joys he looked forward to in Heaven, to her influence. "You will make good use of it, I know," so he wrote, and then with the expressed hope that he should meet her above, ended with "Goodbye."

It was quite a little fortune, and was made the nucleus around which a multitude of kindly deeds for other's comfort and happiness clustered, till Mary used to say it was her fountain of cheer and cave of hid treasures where she had only to wish, to find her desires gratified. But others averred that her loving touch was the secret spell that brought to light all the wonderful wealth of her fairy grotto, and that unselfishness was the constant mantle that gave her such mysterious insight.

Grandma Day ended her work one summer morning, and went gladly "over the river" to meet her John and with him to share Heaven's prefect rest.

Susan's Day's sick room was an "Elim' of rest to all who came within its quiet precincts while she seemed so near the confines of the life to come, that the family often felt it needed the lifting of a curtain to find Heaven all revealed to their vision.

Reader, my task is at an end. If I have but shown to one heart's complete satisfaction that it is only in and through Christ that the soul can be truly strong, pure and peaceful, and that labor for Him goes hand in hand with life's every day duties, and must, like them, be constant, though for a time seemingly fruitless, and all its issues must then be left trustfully with God, I shall feel that I have not written in vain.

Other books by Diane Joy Truitt

For Children

Toby Turtle Rides the Ark
Sammy Serpent Deceives Eve
Daisy Donkey Speaks
Flopsy Frog Survives the Plagues
Leo Lion's Difficult Dinner

Story Resource Book

Doug Parker and the Millennial 2000 Vacuum, and Other Short Stories

A fine collection of 19 short stories, each one being uniquely different, teaching a specific Biblical principle. Can also be used for VBS and family devotions.

Educational Material

Foundations of Holiness

This curriculum is being used by schools as a highschool elective consisting of one-half credit. It covers the basic doctrines Weslyan-Armenian. Other uses are: personal Bible study, group Bible study, ministerial requirement, family devotions and homeschoolers.